Nature Guide t
THE W
COUN

Somerset, Dorset, D ornwall

IAN MERCER

Contents

3 **Introduction**
4 **Geology and Climate**
8 **Habitat Map**
10 **The Coast**
16 **Estuaries**
18 **Moorland**
22 **Farmland**
24 **Woodland**
26 **Rivers and Inland Waters**
28 **Limestone and Chalk**
30 **Heathland**
32 **Somerset Levels**

Common Species of the Countryside and Seashore
33 Introduction
34 Birds
54 Mammals
57 Wild Flowers
79 Butterflies
83 Seashore
89 Trees

Places to Visit
97 Introduction
98 Cornwall
105 Devon
113 Dorset
117 Somerset

122 **Conservation**
123 **Useful Addresses**
Further Reading

124 **Index**
128 **Acknowledgements: Photographers and Artists**

Cover photographs:
Top: Red Fox, Cheddar Pink, Puffins
Centre: Golden Saxifrage, Harvest Mice, Heath Fritillary
Bottom: North Cornwall coast

Title page photograph *(page 1):* Exmoor

"Places to Visit" in Cornwall was written by Tony Thomas Warden of the Field Studies Centre at Slapton Ley, south Devon.

Edited by Rosamund Kidman Cox and Casey Horton
Series Editor: Karen Goaman

Designed by Anne Sharples

The editor wishes to thank the following individuals who helped in the production of this book:
Casey Horton, Felicity Mansfield, Rob Jarman, Mary Fane, Pauline Khng, Anna Makowiecka, Lauris Morgan-Griffiths,
and the following organizations for all their help and guidance: Nature Conservancy Council, Royal Society for the Protection of Birds (Soutn West Office), Cornwall Naturalists' Trust, Devon Trust for Nature Conservation, Dorset Naturalists' Trust, Somerset Trust for Nature Conservation, Royal Albert Memorial Museum, Exeter, National Trust, Forestry Commission

The author dedicates this book to Ben, Tom and Dan, observers all.

Most of the illustrations in the section on pages 33–96, Common Species of the Countryside and Seashore, have been previously published in the Usborne Spotter's Guide series.

First published in 1981 by
Usborne Publishing Limited
20 Garrick Street, London WC2

Printed and bound in Great Britain by
Fakenham Press Limited, Fakenham, Norfolk

Introduction

The south-western peninsula of England offers the visitor a vast variety of natural life and a landscape of many contrasts. Within the four counties of Cornwall, Devon, Somerset and Dorset covered by this book, one can find such extremes as the wave-battered cliffs at Land's End and the soft rich mud of Poole Harbour; the bleak blanket bog and stark tors of Dartmoor and the round chalk downland of Hod Hill and Maiden Castle; the fern-filled woods in narrow Cornish valleys and the wide, wet grassland of the Somerset Levels.

Despite the changes brought about by industry and transport in the last few hundred years, the region nonetheless possesses a wild richness that delights the visitor and resident alike. Badgers trundle through every valley, the call of the Golden Plover is heard in summer on hill tops, and Red Deer venture further afield each year. Buzzards sail serenely over ploughed fields and meadows, orchids of many kinds reappear each spring, and Peregrines still stoop down on their prey in this, England's most western, and possibly most beautiful, region.

▲ Mount St. Michael, Cornwall. Early spring flowers benefit from the warmth of the Gulf Stream, which bathes the whole peninsula.

How to use this Book

The first section of this book, pages 4-32, illustrated with colour photographs and paintings, describes the habitats that are characteristic of the West Country and the animals and plants special to the region. There is a colour map on pages 8-9 showing the main areas in which the habitats occur. Many habitats are closely linked to the geology and climatic conditions of the country, and these features are also described, on pages 4-7.

The middle section of the book, pages 33-96, contains illustrations of over 350 species of animals and plants commonly found in the West Country and over much of Britain. Further details on how to use this section are found on page 33.

The third section of the book, "Places to Visit", found on pages 97-121, consists of a gazetteer containing descriptions of over 150 places of interest. Each county in the West Country has a separate list and map showing the location of the sites. The places described include specific habitats, National Parks, nature reserves, nature trails, good birdwatching points, and some zoos, country parks, gardens, study centres and museums. Further details on how to use this section are found on page 97.

Information such as useful addresses, good reference books, and an index are found at the end of the book. If a species is illustrated, the page number referring to the illustration will appear in bold.

When visiting the countryside, care should be taken to respect the habitats and the wildlife living there. Flowers should not be picked, nesting birds and mammals with young should not be disturbed, and the Country Code, set out on page 122, should always be followed. Some of the problems related to nature conservation in the West Country are also discussed on page 122.

Geology and Climate

The South-West of England is a region of great landscape contrasts. As a peninsula it is 150 miles long, but has some 500 miles of coastline. Britain as a whole is divided into "upland" and "lowland" by a wandering line running from Torquay in the South-West, to Middlesbrough in the North-East. The reason for the division lies in the rocks from which the landscape is carved. West and north of the line the rocks are older, harder, more broken, and often very twisted. To the east, the rocks are softer, less broken and usually lie near the horizontal or slope gently away from it. The south-western end of that line runs from Torquay, via Exeter and Taunton, to Minehead, and then re-appears around the Mendips.

The "Uplands"

To the west of the line, Cornwall, the bulk of Devon and north-western Somerset are largely composed of slates, shales, hard, thin sandstones and some patches of tough limestone. The Mendips are made of a different but equally hard limestone. Embedded in this mixture of rocks are six masses of granite – Dartmoor, Bodmin, St. Austel, Carnmenellis, Carn Brea and Land's End. Exmoor is not granite but its gritty sandstones create similar high moors. Much mining has taken place in this "upland" area and mine waste-tips form part of the scenery, especially in Cornwall. Today only china clay is worked in any quantity.

The coastline round this western half of the peninsula is typically rugged, with cliffs and rocky shores punctuated by sheltered, sandy coves. Much of it is directly attacked by Atlantic waves and nearly all the rock types are exposed on the coast: granites at Land's End, serpentine around the Lizard, limestones at Plymouth and Torbay, and the schists between Bolt Tail and Start Point, are all worth examining.

The "Lowlands"

East of Teignmouth and Minehead, rugged cliffs disappear, long sand or shingle beaches smooth out the coastline, and the cliffs, even where high, carry a good deal of vegetation. These cliffs are often the site of dramatic landslips. The whole landscape of east Devon, Dorset and most of Somerset is developed on a sequence of sandstones, marls, clays and limestones, topped by greensand and chalk; they are

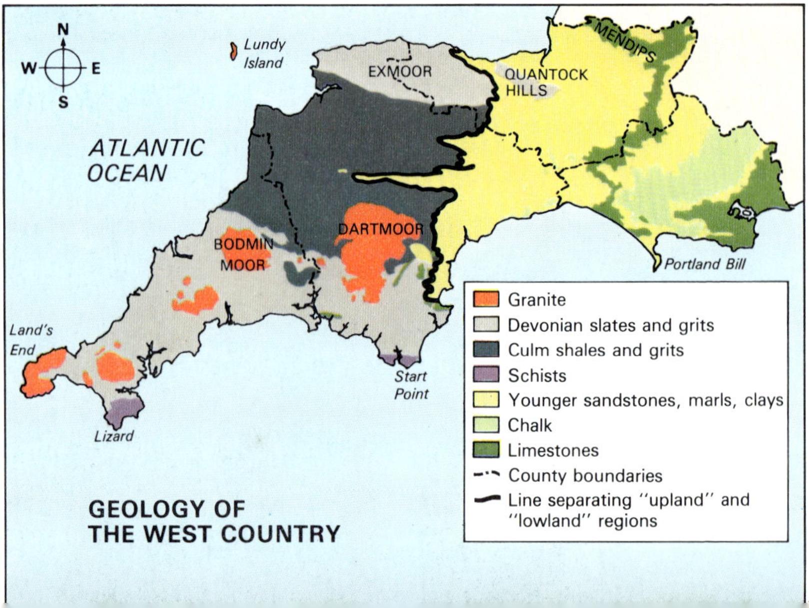

all exposed in the cliffs. Blue Anchor Bay (east end), East Quantoxhead in Somerset, Lyme Regis, Kimmeridge and Swanage in Dorset, are well worth visiting. Most are rich in fossils. Inland, the sandstones, limestone and chalk form the low, rolling hills; marls and clay form the vales.

Changes in Sea Level

The south-western landscape depends for its shapes and patterns on this geological anatomy, and on two recent processes. During the last million years the sea fell from the edges of Dartmoor and Exmoor; it then rose again to its present level. During the fall, wave action "planed off" most hill tops. (Look south-west from Hartland in north Devon, south from Dartmoor, and east from Great Haldon on the A38, and all the skylines are very level.) While this was happening, new radial rivers cut deep narrow valleys. Then the sea rose and drowned the lower ends of those valleys creating the region's 18 superb estuaries, including the Fal, the Tamar, the Exe, and Poole Harbour. At the same time, the rising sea swept before it the shingle of Chesil, Slapton Sands and Westward Ho! into the long, now famous, beaches.

The Ice Age

During the same time-span, the four glaciations of the Ice Age occurred – the last melting beginning only 20,000 years ago. There were no land glaciers in the South-West, but the sea was frozen all around as an arctic climate gripped the landscape.

Freezing and thawing shattered rocks, and in the brief summers, the resulting mixture of rock, sand and clay slithered down every slope. The results of this are the region's massive, blocky granite tors, its jagged, granite western cliff tops, and the very smooth slopes down to the bottom of its valleys.

On the valley bottoms is a coarse, bouldery gravel, best seen on the coastline. Sometimes there is a gravel bench 30 metres (98 feet) high at the foot of the old cliffs – for example, behind Woolacombe Sands and between Start Point and Prawle Point.

The whole region was subjected to the same processes. Soils everywhere have been affected by the down-slope movement of material. Thus sand from hills may be spread over valley clay below, and limestone gravel may lie on acid rock at the foot of slopes.

▼ The hard granite of Land's End, the most westerly point of England, shows jointing (caused by rapid cooling of the rock).

▼ The soft marl and sandstone cliffs near Sidmouth, east Devon. Landslips are common along this stretch of coast.

▲ Schist with large masses of feldspar and quartz. In the background is Prawle Point.

▲ Twisted and tightly folded slate at Boscastle, north Cornwall.

▲ The red sandstone cliffs near Budleigh Salterton are the hardest rocks in east Devon.

▲ Fossils, such as Ammonites, are common in the softer limestones of south Dorset.

▼ Durdle Door, near Lulworth Cove, south Dorset. The limestones and shales in this area have been tightly folded. As the sea erodes the soft rocks, arches, stacks and caves are formed.

▲ Chesil Beach – from Portland to Bridport – is the longest shingle beach in the region.

▲ The extraction of china clay from granite areas is the largest mining industry in the region.

Climate

The South-West peninsula has the mildest climate in Britain. Its coastline is bathed by the Gulf Stream bringing warm water from the Caribbean, and the prevailing south-westerly winds carry moisture-laden air over the whole region. The bulk of the rain falls in the west and on the highest summits. Dartmoor receives over 2540 mm of rain a year on its plateau tops, whereas in east Dorset the rainfall drops to 762 mm. The western moors have a high number of "rain-days", and mist and fog are common. Frosts are rare on the southern Cornish and Devon coastlines and there can be whole winters without snow. Conversely, east and further inland, in north Dorset and south-east Somerset, greater extremes of temperatures and drier air mean that winters and summers are more like those of south-east England.

In the west the wind sweeps across the plateau tops, which can be bleak and are invariably treeless. In contrast, the south-facing sides of sheltered, narrow valleys offer almost sub-tropical sites.

▼ Most of the West Country does not receive a winter covering of snow. However, the moors usually have one or two annual snow falls and in some years spectacular blizzards take the region by surprise.

N
W
E
S
BRIS
Lundy Island
ILFRACOMBE
LYNTON
Morte Point
Baggy Point
BARNSTAPL
BIDEFORD
Hartland Point
Torridge
Bray
Taw
Tamar Lake
BUDE
Bude Bay
Okement
OKEHAMPTON
DE
BOSCASTLE
LAUNCESTON
Lyd
Port Isaac Bay
Bodmin Moor
Pentire Point
Dartmoor
PADSTOW
Dozmary Pool
Siblyback Reservoir
Trevose Head
WADEBRIDGE
Tamar
Camel
BODMIN
Watergate Bay
Lynher
Tavy
Plym
BUCKFASTLEIGH
Fowey
NEWQUAY
LOOE
PLYMOUTH
CORNWALL
ST AUSTELL
Whitesand Bay
Yealm
Erme
Avon
Fal
St Austell Bay
Rame Head
ST IVES
St Ives Bay
TRURO
Bigbury Bay
Stithian's Reservoir
Dodman Point
Eddystone
Bolt Head
FALMOUTH
PENZANCE
HELSTON
Loe Pool
Helford
Falmouth Bay
Mount's Bay
Manacle Point
ENGLIS
Land's End
Lizard Point
Kilometres
0
10
20
30
40
50
60
0
10
20
30
Miles

CHANNEL
Bridgwater Bay
BURNHAM-ON-SEA
CHEDDAR
MINEHEAD
Axe
WELLS
Somerset Levels
Quantocks
Brue
BRIDGWATER
Wimbleball Reservoir
Cary
Parrett
TAUNTON
Tone
SOMERSET
YEOVIL
Sherborne Lake
Tiverton Canal
Culm
CRICKET ST THOMAS
Otter
DORSET
Stour
HONITON
Yarty
Axe
Exe
Char
BOURNEMOUTH
Frome
LYME REGIS
Poole Harbour
SIDMOUTH
DORCHESTER
Lyme Bay
Radipole Lake
Chesil Beach
Teign
EXMOUTH
SWANAGE
WEYMOUTH
Durlston Head
St Alban's Head
NEWTON ABBOT
Bill of Portland
TORBAY
DARTMOUTH
Start Point
HANNEL
HABITATS OF THE WEST COUNTRY
Moorland
Heathland
Somerset Levels
Farmland and woodland
Rocky shore
Shingle or sand
Sand dunes
Saltmarsh and mudflats
Cliffs
National park boundary
County boundary
Canal

The Coast

Much of the length of the long south-western coastline is accounted for by innumerable inlets, bays and estuaries. The great variety of rocks, and the variation in their exposure to the Atlantic, has resulted in a coastline of great diversity and beauty. All types of coastal habitats occur – rocky and sandy shores, shingle, sand dunes, estuaries and saltmarshes – each with its characteristic community of plants and animals.

The north coast of Cornwall and Devon is more exposed to wave action than is the south coast, and therefore has more cliffs and a less accessible shore. On the south coast, from the Lizard in Cornwall, to Start Point in Devon, there is more shore, usually rocky. Shingle or sandy shores dominate between Start and Portland in Dorset.

Cliff Plants

Many parts of the South-West coast have been designated as Areas of Outstanding Natural Beauty. Colourful plants, such as Thrift, Sea Campion and Rock Samphire are common, even on vertical cliffs. Bramble, Bracken, Gorse and Heather cover the more gentle slopes, and in places Blackthorn has been shaped by onshore winds into impenetrable, thorny thickets. Many of the cliffs, particularly along the south coast, are sites for rare or unusual plants such as Broomrape, Three-cornered Leek and Wild Cabbage.

On the cliff tops, common plants include Thrift, Bird's Foot Trefoil, Alexanders, Thyme and Wild Teasel. Many butterflies occur on the south coast cliffs and there is a good chance of spotting summer migrants, such as the Clouded Yellow and Painted Lady.

Cliff Birds

Vertical cliffs with convenient ledges, particularly along the Cornish and north Devon coast, are nesting sites for sea birds. Guillemots and Razorbills breed on stacks off the north Cornish coast west of Boscastle, on the cliffs of Woody Bay near Ilfracombe and at Berry Head in Torbay; they are also found, with Puffins, on the island of Lundy. Kittiwakes and Fulmars have spread rapidly from north-west Cornwall and Torbay during the last 20 years, while Shags, Cormorants and various gulls may be seen all round the coast. Jackdaws, Ravens and Kestrels may also nest on the cliffs.

▼ Cliff-top turf: Thrift (*front*), Ox-eye Daisy (*centre*), and Kidney Vetch (*background*).

▲ Tree Mallow is common on the coast. It grows very tall when undisturbed, for example on rocky headlands and islands.

▲ Rock Samphire grows on cliffs, and rocky places at the base of cliffs. Its fleshy leaves retain moisture and help it to withstand drought.

▲ Hottentot Fig. A South African plant, naturalized on frost-free cliff faces in south Devon, Cornwall and the Channel Islands.

▲ Golden Samphire can be found on the south coast and on the north Cornish coast. It grows on cliffs, shingle and sometimes in saltmarsh.

▲ Spring Squill. Locally common in the region, it grows on short turf on cliff tops and slopes.

▲ Sea Lavender grows in saltmarsh, turf, and on well-drained slopes at the cliff foot.

▼ Six-spot Burnet Moth, feeding on Sea Holly. A day-flying moth, it may be seen in summer.

▼ The Peregrine Falcon has returned to the south-western cliffs within the last decade.

▲ Grey Seals are often seen singly, just offshore from rocky headlands. Remote sea caves are the only breeding sites in the West Country.

▲ Guillemots nest on cliff ledges at Berry Head, Woody Bay, on Lundy and on a number of Cornish cliffs. They winter at sea.

▲ Razorbills nest in colonies on cliff ledges in Cornwall and on Lundy. They winter at sea.

▼ Cormorants are widespread on the coast, but they nest at only a few sites in the region.

▲ Schools of Dolphins are common offshore in the summer. At high water they may be seen quite far up some of the region's estuaries.

▲ Fulmars have spread rapidly along the coasts of the South-West. Long swooping glides, made with stiff wings, help to identify them.

▼ Puffins nest in old rabbit holes on ancient cliff slopes. Lundy is their south-western stronghold. They winter at sea.

Rocky Shores

In the "hard" coast areas, sheltered rocky shores have the greatest number of seaweeds and animals.

At the top of the shore, just above high water mark but splashed by the waves, lichens cover the rock, making a distinct yellow zone. Different species of brown seaweeds mark the tidal levels down the beach. At the top of the shore, submerged only at high tide, is the Channelled Wrack, then Spiral Wrack, followed by Knotted Wrack. This seaweed grows a bladder, or "knot" every year, so you can tell the age of each plant. It is sensitive to wave attack and thus is an indicator of sheltered shores. If the shore is more exposed, Bladder Wrack will take the place of the Knotted Wrack. Near the bottom of the shore is a narrow band of Serrated Wrack. Finally, right at the bottom of the shore, and only exposed at the lowest spring tides, are the great leathery straps of the Oarweeds.

Some of the more beautiful sea animals can be found in this submerged area, such as Sea Slugs, live Cowries, Sea Squirts, Blue-rayed Limpets and Sponges.

As you go from sheltered to exposed areas of the shore, Barnacles take the place of seaweeds. These animals are stuck down head first onto the rock and use their feet to catch food moving past. They need rough water to provide a continuous fresh supply of food. Mussels may accompany them, and so may the predatory Dog Whelks. Periwinkles can always be found in more sheltered areas, and where rock pools are permanent, Anemones, Crabs and shore fish such as Blennies will be present.

▲ Dog Whelks are common on rocky shores. They feed on Mussels and Barnacles using their tongues to drill holes in the shells.

▼ South-western rocky shores are often steep and irregular, like this one at Hurlstone Point in Somerset. Note the zones of Barnacles.

▲ Blennies cause the splash you hear as you approach a rock pool. They spend some time sitting out of the water on their front fins.

▲ There are many kinds of Starfish living below low water mark; after gales they are often stranded on the shore.

▲ The Sea Hare is a type of Sea Slug (a mollusc); it swims slowly and gracefully, by waving the frills around its "foot".

▲ Lobster fishing, a major industry in the West Country at the start of the century, is now only a part-time occupation.

▼ Logan Rock Beach, Cornwall. A typical sandy bay, attractive to humans, but not to animals.

Sandy Shores

The best sandy beaches are on the north coasts of Cornwall and Devon where Atlantic rollers provide a regular supply and removal of sand. The sand is very mobile under water so few creatures can live in it. However, at low water mark, wave action is more limited and Razorshells, Starfish, some burrowing bivalve molluscs and the odd Sea Urchin may be found.

▲ A large hole in sand or mud indicates the presence of a Razorshell (a mollusc).

Sand Dunes and Shingle Beaches

When sand dries during low tides it may be picked up by the wind and blown inland. Dune systems form in this way. Sand dunes occur at Braunton and Dawlish Warren in Devon, and at Studland in Dorset, with many smaller versions at the back of north Cornish beaches. These are fascinating places, with "yellow" fore-dunes carrying Marram Grass and plants such as Sea Holly, and "grey" dunes behind them, where a kind of heath develops. Between dune crests there are damp dune hollows called slacks where orchids may grow; damp scrub will develop in these slacks.

Shingle beaches occur at Slapton and Chesil. Fine shingle has some of the characteristics of sand dunes and similar plants inhabit both. At Slapton the pioneer plants are Sea Spurge, Rest-harrow, Yellow Horned Poppy, Sea Couch Grass and Sea Mayweed. The amount of shell in the shingle attracts limestone plants such as Viper's Bugloss; this is also a common plant on sand dunes. On both dunes and shingle, scrub may develop which increases the value of the place for birds. Terns, Plovers and Oystercatchers nest in sandy hollows or on the shingle at Chesil, and many birds rest here during migration.

▲ Fore-dunes at Braunton Burrows, north Devon. Marram Grass anchors drifting sand and helps to stabilize the dune system.

▲ Yellow Horned Poppy is a pioneer plant of shingle beaches. It has very long seed pods.

▼ Viper's Bugloss (*left*) grows on shingle and on sand dunes. Marsh Helleborine (*centre*) and Round-leaved Wintergreen (*right*) grow in the damp hollows between dunes, called dune slacks.

Estuaries

Estuaries are the lowest reaches of rivers drowned by the sea, either because the land has sunk or because the sea level has risen recently. Most rivers on the south coast have an estuary, since the sea level here has been gradually rising for some 20,000 years.

Most of the estuaries of Cornwall and west Devon have steep sides and narrow, branching creeks. They contrast with the estuaries in the softer rocks east of the Exe, such as the Otter, Axe and Char. These estuaries are almost completely silted up and are surrounded by large areas of salt-marsh and wet fields.

Estuaries are biologically very rich. All the material that the streams and rain-wash carry off the surrounding landscape accumulates in the estuary. Twice daily fresh food comes in from the sea as the tides go in and out. An estuary can thus support a vast array of soft-bodied and shelly animals which in turn help support a fish and bird population greater than that of any other habitat.

The birds are the most obvious sign of the richness of estuaries, but a walk along the tideline or on the mudflats will reveal

▲ The Kingsbridge Estuary, south Devon.

▲ Redshank and Dunlin are common on every estuary, throughout the year. Grey Plover (in the foreground) breed in the Arctic; they can be seen from autumn to spring.

▲ A winter flock of Avocets occurs annually on the Exe and Tamar estuaries.

▲ Wigeon may be seen in huge numbers on the Exe and Tamar estuaries every winter.

▼ The Exe estuary is a very important wintering area for Black-tailed Godwits.

▼ Brent Geese come onto the Exe estuary each winter to graze the Eel Grass on the mudflats.

signs of all the animals living under the mud. Holes with casts may be the homes of Lugworms, holes without casts may be the homes of Ragworms. The presence of Tellin, Cockles and Sand Gapers in the mud can be detected by empty shells on the surface. The edges of estuaries are essentially the most sheltered seashores and where they are rocky they support seaweeds and animals characteristic of sheltered shores.

Only plants that can tolerate salty water, for example Glasswort, Cord-grass and Seablite, will grow in the mudflats at the sides of the estuary. Behind this area, where proper saltmarsh has formed, more colourful plants such as Sea Aster and Sea Lavender will be found growing.

The most common waders in the West Country are Dunlin, Knot, Ringed Plover, Redshank, Bar-tailed Godwit, Oystercatcher and Curlew. Heron, Wigeon and Cormorant also feed in the estuaries, and the smaller, sheltered estuaries are the winter home for Spotted Redshank and Greenshank.

The narrow, steep-sided estuaries of Cornwall and south Devon do not have much mud exposed at low water. It is often difficult to reach the small areas where the birds feed. Estuaries where the mudflats are wider at low tide provide greater security for birds. However, here it is difficult to observe them, except at a distance, since they are very wary and must be approached across the mud without benefit of cover.

Mud-feeding waders and other birds have a tidal routine rather than a day and night one, so they roost at high tide at the edges of the estuary. They are then best observed from accessible sites which offer cover – for example, man-made features such as sea walls.

During spring tides (which occur every new and full moon) high water may force the birds away from the shore to nearby fields. The months of May, June and July are also less profitable times for birdwatching, since this is when most birds will leave the estuaries to breed .

The Exe, Tamar, Taw/Torridge, Parrett, Poole and Fal estuaries offer the best opportunities for birdwatching. The Exe is particularly good, as it is a protected bird sanctuary and accessible.

▲ Flatfish like the Flounder may be seen on the sandy and gravelly bottoms of estuaries.

▲ Brittle Stars, closely related to Starfish, prefer the stony shores and rocks of estuaries.

▼ Glasswort is a common pioneer colonizer of saltmarsh and brackish dune slacks.

▼ Sea Aster can be dense enough to give an all-over pink sheen to a saltmarsh "meadow".

Moorland

Three large moors lie in the upland area of the peninsula, west of the geological dividing line that runs from Minehead to Torbay. They all have similar vegetation and, given differences in size, similar populations of animals, so the following description of Dartmoor applies generally to all moorland areas in the West Country.

Dartmoor is the largest moor, centred on two high moorland plateaux; but the whole area also includes woods, plantations, rivers, pools, fields, walls, hedges, farms, and villages. It is this combination of habitats which makes the National Park such a fascinating wildlife observatory.

Dartmoor moorland has two summit blanket bogs. Blanket bog is a peat formation covering huge areas of undulating plateau top. Unlike valley bog it contains both wet and relatively dry places. On Dartmoor these bogs cover some 1,200 hectares (30,000 acres), and in places the peat is 3.5 metres (12 feet) deep, forming dangerous mires. Cotton Grass, Purple Moor Grass and Deer Grass dominate the bog proper with sheets of Sphagnum Moss in the wettest places, and islands of Heather, Sheep's Fescue Grass, Bent Grass and even Bracken in the driest. Snipe, Lapwing and Red Grouse are scarce breeders in this area, and a few pairs of Golden Plover and Dunlin breed in the heart of the northern plateau.

Away from the bog, the dry slopes carry Ling (heather), grasses, Bracken and Gorse and, where this vegetation is not too tall, small plants such as Milkwort, Tormentil and Heath Bedstraw add tiny spots of colour. In late summer the slopes are full of colour with great patches of flowering Bell Heather, Ling and Western Gorse.

Both dry and wet heath have dense populations of Skylarks and Meadow Pipits, while Bracken and Gorse attract Stonechats and Whinchats. Buzzards, Kestrels and Adders are common predators. Short-eared Owls and Hen Harriers occasionally hunt over the area. The granite tors that punctuate the skyline are lookout posts for Buzzards and are nesting

▼ Granite tors and the ponies are the two unforgettable things about Dartmoor. The ponies are not wild; they are rounded up once a year – the "drift" – and the foals are sold off by the owners.

▲ Introduced Red Grouse are present in small numbers on Dartmoor and Exmoor.

▲ A few pairs of Golden Plover breed on the remote high moorlands of Dartmoor.

▲ Stonechats are usually seen perching on the topmost sprigs of Gorse bushes. They feed mainly on the ground.

▲ The Ring Ouzel often breeds in old quarries or ruined buildings. On moorland, look at every "Blackbird" twice to see if it is a Ring Ouzel.

▲ Dartmoor is the national stronghold of the Wheatear. It nests in holes in rocks and walls.

▲ A few pairs of Merlin, the smallest falcon, have bred on Exmoor and Dartmoor in recent years.

▼ Ravens are carrion feeders. They nest early in the West Country, in the upland areas, on cliffs and in other rocky places.

▼ Buzzards are the largest predators in the region, common throughout Devon, Cornwall and Somerset, on the coast and inland.

sites for Ravens and Kestrels. The clitter (fallen boulders) around many of the large tors is the favourite haunt of the Wheatear, whose population is more dense on Dartmoor than anywhere else in England.

Woodlands on Dartmoor

The coniferous plantations on the moor have their own special wildlife. Crossbills and Redpolls would not breed on Dartmoor without the plantations. Three plantations are linked to reservoirs, and this combination of trees and water possibly benefits species such as the Heron.

Broadleaved woodlands on valley sides consist mainly of Oak, Ash, Beech, Rowan, Silver Birch and Sycamore. Mosses, Bilberry, and ferns cover the woodland floor along with shade-loving plants such as Enchanter's Nightshade and Wood Sorrel.

Wood Warblers, Redstarts and, increasingly, Pied Flycatchers occur with Tits, Nuthatches, Treecreepers and Woodpeckers. Valley woods straddle rivers, so waterside birds – Dippers, Grey Wagtails and Sandpipers – can almost be regarded as woodland birds.

Badgers, Foxes, Stoats and Weasels live in the woods as well as on the open moor, as do the woodland deer – Red, Fallow and Roe. The Teign and Dart Valley woods are the most extensive in the region, and are accessible from almost every road bridge.

▼ Red Deer have spread from Exmoor and Great Haldon into wooded valleys and over Dartmoor.

▲ Exmoor. Heather is diminishing on most moorlands, probably because over-management encourages Purple Moor Grass and Bracken.

▲ Snipe breed in valley bogs and in damp hollows on most moors in the West Country.

▲ Dippers breed on all streams more than 8 km (5 miles) long in the West Country.

▼ Grey Wagtails nest beside fast-flowing streams. They feed on insects near the water.

▲ The Emperor Moth is a moorland species. It flies by day in June and July. The eggs (*left*) are laid on heather, on which the caterpillar feeds (*centre*). It forms a cocoon (*right*) in August.

▲ Adders live on moor and heath – including cliff-top heath. They are sensitive to vibrations and will move away if footsteps approach.

▲ Common Lizards are present on the drier, sunnier sites throughout the moorland. They can be seen warming themselves on sunny days.

▲ The Round-leaved Sundew catches flies with its sticky hairs. It is found in boggy areas.

▲ Bog Asphodel occurs in wet acidic places on moors and heaths. It flowers in summer.

▼ Grazed moorland is studded with Tormentil flowers in summer (*right*). In places Bilberry, in flower (*centre*) takes over from heather. Heather and Gorse may carry the parasitic leafless Dodder (*left*).

Farmland

Farmland makes up more than three-quarters of Somerset, Dorset and Devon, and nearly two-thirds of Cornwall. Changes in farming patterns occur as you go up the peninsula; they reflect both geological and climatic changes. The small, rough fields of west Cornwall and north-west Devon change to rich pastureland in east Cornwall and south Devon, then to the red, even richer soils of east Devon and Somerset. The limestones of Dorset support more and more ploughland in an easterly direction.

As farmland developed, species had time to adapt to the new environment and take advantage of the changes. Strips of low, scrubby woodland, left as hedges between fields, soon became the breeding sites, look-out posts or hiding places of woodland birds and other animals.

West Cornwall has a very dense network of narrow valleys and valley-side woods; it also has a lot of rough grazing pasture that supports many animals and plants. East Cornwall, Devon and west Somerset have an intricate landscape of small hills and valleys, woods, hedges and scattered farmsteads, knitted together by a network of lanes. Most lanes have sunk below the level of the fields through the wear and tear of centuries and the gullying of rain-wash, before being covered with tarmac in the last 50 years

The term hedge is a general one, used to describe a variety of fences, stone walls, beech hedges, bushy lowland hedges and roadside banks. Hedges reflect both geology and human history. The stone walls of granite, schist, slate and limestone occur on each side of the moors, on the blunt peninsula of south Devon, in Portland, Purbeck and the Mendips. East Cornwall and the Devon hinterland carry great earth banks "nine feet at the base, four and a half at summit, stoned to four feet at the side, and the top planted with withies and other shrubs", according to an eighteenth-century recipe. Many of these hedges are even older – possibly Anglo-Saxon; they offer superb burrowing and nesting sites, as well as cover.

The beech hedges of Exmoor are rather similar in their general form, but less rich as habitats. True lowland hedges, consisting of bushes growing at field level, are found in a few places in Somerset and east Devon. Roadside hedges, where spraying or cutting has not been too devastating, have a continuous succession of flowers from spring to autumn.

▼ Hedgerow flowers (*left to right, from top*): Dog Rose, Honeysuckle; Tufted Vetch, Hogweed, Red Campion, Foxglove, Meadowsweet, Hemp Agrimony; Red Campion, Herb Robert.

▲ Farmland broken up by hedges and woods.

▲ Barn Owls can be seen at dusk over farmland.

▲ Migrant flocks of Fieldfares feed in the fields from late autumn to early spring.

▲ The Cirl Bunting needs warm, sheltered conditions. South Devon is its national stronghold.

▲ Primroses on a Devon roadside bank.

▲ Red Valerian is very common on walls.

▼ Stone wall with Common Polypody, Biting Stonecrop, Pennywort (*centre*) and Ivy-leaved Toadflax.

Woodland

Woodland is the natural vegetation of England. All open land, apart from blanket bogs and other wetlands, is the result of woodland clearance. The remaining woods exist today either where it has proved useful to leave them, or where they have been planted since the original clearance. Far more woods are found on slopes and valley sides than on flat ground. Newer plantations may be found on flatter ground where the poor quality of the land – as suggested by the presence of heath – makes it unsuitable for other agricultural purposes.

Deciduous Woodland

Oakwood dominates on steep valley sides in Devon, Cornwall and west Somerset. For centuries it was managed by coppicing – cutting stems from a root-stock every 10-15 years to provide wood for poles, firewood and fence posts, and bark for tanning. A few woods are still coppiced in Somerset and Dorset.

Oakwood is well lit and therefore contains many species of plants. Bluebells, Woodrush and Dog's Mercury dominate on heavier soils; Bilberry is common in the oakwoods of the hills. Enchanter's Nightshade and some Hogweed occur at the sides of woodland trails. The edges of the wood and its internal clearings are the favoured sites of insects and birds. The Speckled Wood and the Silver-washed Fritillary are fairly common butterflies and the White Admiral can be found in some of the larger woods. All three species of woodpecker occur, while the more open oak copses on the edges of the hills are currently the scene of an expansion in the breeding population of hole-nesting birds, especially the Pied Flycatcher and the Redstart.

Extensive blocks of oakwood remain in the larger valleys of the Dart, Exe, Tamar, Fal, Taw and Torridge. While those near the south coast have an almost tropical luxuriance, on the whole the woods have been neglected and regular "weeding" is necessary to prevent other tree species such as Beech and Sycamore taking over.

Beechwood occurs on the hillsides on the softer limestones, particularly in north-central Dorset. Beech trees are handsome but few plants can survive in their shade; they are also shallow-rooted and so compete with ground plants.

The harder limestones now and then

▼ Bringing the woodlands of the South-West back into good health demands felling and replanting of small blocks which must be hand-weeded, in this case by volunteers at Slapton, Devon.

bear pure ashwoods, especially in the Mendip valleys. Lime soil and good lighting combine to produce perhaps the richest woodland ground flora of the region, including Hellebores, Lily of the Valley and Wild Madder.

Coniferous Woodland

Coniferous plantations dominate in Dorset on former heathland. They also occupy upland and valley-side sites on the fringes of Dartmoor and Exmoor, and some are found on the heavier clays of mid-Devon and north Cornwall. These woods are favoured by birds such as Goldcrests, Crossbills and Redpolls. No ground plants grow in the dark, densely-planted forests. However, the trees are subject to rotational harvesting, so there are always some clearings and young plantations to be found in any large block.

Mammals

The four types of woodland are the home of Britain's largest land mammals – Foxes, Badgers and Deer. A wood is warmer, darker and damper and has more cover than any other habitat, and is therefore an important refuge in the cultivated countryside. The network of small copses and hedges provide equally important, temporary shelter. Both Roe and Fallow Deer occur throughout the region but Fallow Deer are most likely to be seen. Red Deer are spreading from an Exmoor stronghold, and the Quantocks, Haldon Hills and Dartmoor are now showing increases. Deer, Badgers and Foxes will be seen if deliberately watched for. However, it is far easier, and just as fascinating, to look for the tracks and other signs left by woodland animals.

▲ Woodland, Exmoor. The most extensive broad-leaved woodland in the region is now on steep valley sides, where farming is impossible.

▲ The rare Heath Fritillary is now restricted to a few sites in the West Country. It inhabits open woodland and woodland edges.

▲ Redpolls are common in old coniferous plantations, but they also occur on heathland.

▼ Woodland mammals are rarely seen, but evidence of their presence is always there: a Squirrel's feeding place (*left*); old bedding outside a Badger's sett (*centre*); marks made by Deer antlers (*right*).

Rivers and Inland Waters

The main rivers of the area arise on the high ground near the north coast of Devon and Cornwall or on Dartmoor. These are also the areas with the highest rainfall. Both the Exe and Tamar, the largest rivers, flow right across to the south coast. Somerset and Dorset are largely drained to their own coastlines.

The rivers of Devon and Cornwall are acid (nutrient-poor) to neutral. Their freshwater populations, though varied, lack the better specimens of Brown Trout found in the alkaline waters of chalk and limestone streams. Nevertheless, where the rivers are large enough, the migratory activities of Salmon and Sea Trout may be observed from August to December. They may be seen jumping at the weirs and basking in pools in August; in November and December they reach upper gravel beds of rivers where they will spawn.

Natural lakes are rare and, except for Dozmary Pool on Bodmin Moor, are confined to the coastline where shingle ridges have trapped lagoons above sea level. Slapton Ley in south Devon is the largest lake but small lakes also occur at Beesands, Loe Bar near Helston and one or two minor Cornish sites. At other lake sites, land has been naturally and artificially reclaimed and now only small reed beds remain.

Slapton Ley, with some 82 hectares (200 acres) of open water, is by far the largest lake in the area and is a rewarding place to visit. It has a rich flora, with Reeds, Reedmace, Bulrushes, Purple Loosestrife, and Yellow Iris fringing much of its shore. Water-lilies, Water Crowfoot and Bistort float on its surface. Wildfowl congregate in large numbers during hard winters. Reed, Sedge, and recently Cetti's Warblers breed there in summer. The lake's large insect population supports these birds and also the vast number of Pike, Perch, Rudd and Eel.

In contrast, the number of artificial lakes in the West Country is high. Most of them are reservoirs, all built in the last 100 years. There are more reservoirs in the hills than in the lowlands – eight on Dartmoor alone. Upland reservoirs are not rich in

▼ Nearly all the common waterside plants can be seen along the banks of the Tiverton Canal, Devon.

wildlife owing to their acidity, steep shores and newness. Conversely, the lowland lakes are richer and have more wildfowl. Stithians and Siblyback in Cornwall, and the Tamar Lake on the Devon/Cornwall border are all especially good for bird-watching. The Tamar Lake has a large variety of breeding and migrant wildfowl, and in the reed beds the occasional Water Rail may be seen. The tracks and spraints (droppings) of Otters may be seen at the side of the lake, though, as in the rest of the region, the Otter is now a rare animal. Much more common are Mink, descendants of animals that escaped from the Mink farms of the 1950's.

The lakes created by country gentlemen – at Sherborne in Dorset, and Cricket St Thomas in Somerset – are rich in wildlife, as are the canals and leats (water channels) of past industrial activities. Somerset has the longest remaining canal, and the Tiverton Canal in Devon is a country park and nature reserve. These stretches of water provide an interesting link between the still lakes and fast-flowing rivers, having some characteristics of both.

▲ The Otter was once common on all rivers. It is now restricted to a few undisturbed coastal sites and quiet stretches of river.

▲ Mink, often mistaken for Otters, are now found along all waterways in the region.

▲ Kingfishers are more common east of Exeter. In Cornwall and west Devon, nest sites are rare.

▼ Common waterside plants: Yellow Flag (*left*), Purple Loosestrife (*centre*), Water Crowfoot (*right*).

Limestone and Chalk

The limestones fall into two categories: the hard rocks of the Mendips, Torbay, and Plymouth, and the softer chalk and limestones of east Devon, Dorset and Somerset. There is much more of this softer chalk and limestone covering larger areas – more than half of Dorset carries calcareous soils. However, the hard limestone outcrops in south Devon are small and, with one exception, coastal.

The hard limestone outcrops bear the range of flora typical of lowland limestone areas: this includes Horseshoe Vetch, Wall Pennywort, Old Man's Beard, Dropwort and Biting Stonecrop. The south-western position of the outcrops explains why they also carry a few species which otherwise only occur in southern Europe. One example is the White Rockrose of Berry Head at the south end of Torbay.

The inland limestone at Buckfastleigh and Ashburton – quarried by the Victorians as marble – has an intricate cave system which, among other things, houses a collection of inter-glacial mammal fossils such as Hyenas and Sabre-Toothed Tigers. It is also one of the few roosting sites of the rare Greater Horseshoe Bat.

The Mendips form the largest single block of hard limestone in the region, and are the only example of the type of limestone (Carboniferous) which, further north, forms the bastions of the Pennines. Cave systems occur here which, like those at Buckfastleigh and Ashburton, house both fossils and bats. In a few places the limestone summits bear short turf with its associated rich flora. The Ox-eye Daisy is conspicuous in summer, Sea Campion occurs amongst the inland plants, and the White Rockrose is present at the seaward end. One of the most beautiful plants in this area is the rare Blue Gromwell. The gorges, notably at Cheddar Gorge, have many rare or localised flowers on the ledges and screes, such as Cheddar Pink, Bloody Cranesbill and Lady's Mantle.

All the downland of Dorset and also the dry valleys in the east of the region are situated on the softer chalk and limestones. The basic community of flowers, birds and butterflies found here is common to all limey soils in Britain. The richness of the soil indicates its value to the farmer. As a result, downland is increasingly rare, since arable work replaces sheep grazing which created and maintained the short rich turf. There is now a strong need to make the remaining downland areas nature reserves.

▼ Maiden Castle, Dorset, a prehistoric fort. The vegetation is typical of grazed chalk downlands.

Where true downland still occurs, as at Hod Hill or on Maiden Castle in Dorset, it is best enjoyed by sitting down and carefully examining a small patch of ground: the number of species to be found is startling. Superb little plants such as Salad Burnet, Squinancywort, Purging Flax, Hoary Plantain and Harebell abound.

Where Rabbits are scarce and sheep cannot reach, the small amount of grazing allows taller flowers to grow. This is where you will find Clustered Bellflower, Horseshoe Vetch and Musk Thistle. A careful search may reveal orchids including the commoner species – Spotted and Pyramidal – and the less common Butterfly and Bee Orchids. Even Frog, Early Spider and Man Orchids can be found in the region.

The limestone plants are accompanied by typical populations of snails, grasshoppers and butterflies, especially skippers and blues, and including such rarities as the Lulworth Skipper. Anthills are common and provide food for Green Woodpeckers. Skylarks are as common here as on moorland and heath. Purbeck, Portland and Maiden Castle are good places to see Corn Buntings.

▲ Cheddar Gorge, Somerset. A rich community of plants grow on the limestone ledges. The tree in the foreground is Whitebeam.

▲ Greater Horseshoe Bats roost in limestone caves in Devon and Somerset.

▲ Limestone, with its special flora, also has special insects such as the Chalkhill Blue.

▲ The White Rockrose grows on the limestones of the Mendips and at Berry Head in Devon.

▼ Downland flowers: Pyramidal Orchid (*left*), Clustered Bellflower (*centre*), Bee Orchid (*right*).

Heathland

The "lowland" heaths of the West Country all lie east of Dartmoor. Some, as in the Bovey Basin near Newton Abbot, are physically low-lying, but most of them are situated on plateau tops. The latter include the commons of east Devon and the heaths of Dorset.

In some senses, heaths are replaced in the upland areas of west Devon and Cornwall by moorland, which has a similar range of plants and animals, though small areas of "upland" heath do occur on the Cornish coast and on the Quantocks.

Heathland is the direct result of natural woodland clearance exposing thin, acid, sandy or gravelly soils, only capable of supporting a poor vegetation. (Moors have nutrient-poor, acid, peaty soils.) Heath has little value as arable land and thus was first used as common grazing. Grazing and burning have maintained it since then. Unmanaged and ungrazed heath slowly reverts to scrub of Birch and Sallow and, if left long enough, to thin Oak woodland. It is now often regarded as wasteland and is therefore prey to afforestation, golf course developers, military manoeuvres, industrial development and those who are interested in the sand and gravel beneath. Heath is also particularly vulnerable to fires in times of drought. It is a disappearing habitat throughout southern Britain and considerable efforts are being made to preserve it by all the conservation bodies.

Heathers, mostly Ling, but also Bell Heather and Cross-leaved Heath, dominate the true heaths. Bracken may take over on better drained and deeper soils. The tall European Gorse often grows at the edges while the squat, prickly cushions of Western Gorse mix with the heathers on some slopes. Other plants are scattered but regular – notably Milkwort, Lousewort, Tormentil and Heath Bedstraw. Bilberry is present in a few places. Wetter places sometimes carry Dwarf Willow and Bog Myrtle and the occasional Heath Spotted Orchid. The rare Dorset Heath has its base in Purbeck; otherwise it occurs only in a few places in Devon.

As on heather moorland, the Emperor Moth and Fox Moth are typical. Grasshoppers, Bumble-bees and occasionally

▼ Coastal heathland, near Land's End, Cornwall, showing Western Gorse and Bell Heather.

butterflies such as the Grayling are common, and many species of spiders and beetles favour this dry, open habitat. Adders, and, in the wetter places, Grass Snakes, are also common on the heaths.

Meadow Pipits, Linnets and Stonechats are the commonest birds – the Pipit is prey to the snakes when in the nest and is also the commonest host to the Cuckoo. The Nightjar may be heard calling at dusk or dawn, and in summer the rare Hobby and Montagu's Harrier are occasionally seen. The rarest bird is the Dartford Warbler: Dorset heathland, along with the New Forest, is its only British stronghold.

▲ The commonest "small, brown bird" of heath and moor is the Meadow Pipit.

▲ The very rare Dartford Warbler lives in Gorse thickets in Dorset and east Devon.

▲ Montagu's Harrier has occasionally bred in the region. Often seen in spring and autumn.

▲ West Country heaths often support large areas of Dwarf Gorse and Ling; here Dorset Heath (in the foreground) accompanies them.

▲ Two male Sand Lizards (males are greener than females). This reptile is rare in the region, being confined to a few heaths in Dorset.

▼ Nightjars call at dusk on some heathlands.

▼ Tiger Beetles are common on heathland.

Somerset Levels

The Somerset Levels are a nationally important wetland, occupying the great plain between the Quantock Hills and the Mendips. The plain was originally a large, shallow sea inlet. Since the last Ice Age, the inlet gradually silted up. Fens (alkaline, or neutral, marshland) developed and over several thousand years peat formed, thus raising the level of the land. In the centre of these fens two raised, acid peat bogs formed.

Since the Middle Ages drainage of the fens has created farmland. A pattern of wet meadows has emerged, each meadow "fenced" off by ditches called rhines. A rich flora provides excellent grazing pasture and supports many invertebrate animals and a large number of breeding birds. Curlew, Redshank, Snipe and Lapwing fill the air with superb sounds; Sedge Warblers, Whinchats and Yellow Wagtails are common along the rhine margins, and Short-eared Owls and Hobbies occasionally breed in the area. Large numbers of pollarded Willows grow beside the rhines providing nest places for Little Owls and Redstarts; flowering plants such as Purple Loosestrife and Meadowsweet grow at the rhine edges, and a great variety of plants and insects live in the rhine waters.

However, farmers are under pressure to "improve" the pastures. More efficient drainage dries out the meadows and reduces the amount of winter flooding on the Levels. This in turn reduces feeding areas for huge numbers of waders and wildfowl – Golden Plover, Snipe, Bewick's Swans, White-fronted Geese – that arrive in winter. Ploughing, fertilizing and regular cleaning of the rhines also destroys the wetland plant and animal communities.

Peat digging threatens the area. The central bogs were traditionally worked for peat (used as a fuel). Abandoned peat cuttings have a wet heath vegetation with heather on the ridges and Sphagnum Moss, Sundew and Bog Asphodel in the trenches. Wet woodland has developed on long abandoned cuttings. However, commercial digging for horticultural peat is destroying the few remaining areas of bog and removing the heath and woodland on the old cuttings, without allowing time for regrowth of the vegetation.

▲ Rhines (the drainage ditches between meadows) are rich in plant and animal life.

▲ The peat of the Somerset Levels is dug both by small firms and on a huge commercial scale.

▼ The Royal Fern (*left*) and Greater Bladderwort (*centre*) are two of the rare plants of the Levels. The Southern Marsh Orchid (*right*) grows in the wet meadows.

Common Species of the Countryside and Seashore

Some of Britain's animals and plants can be found only in certain regions, or are more easily found in some areas than in others. Living alongside these rare or local species are, of course, many animals and plants which are fairly widespread throughout the country. The more common species of British birds, wild flowers, trees, butterflies, mammals and seashore animals are illustrated on the following pages. These illustrations form a basic field guide to the majority of the regions in Britain.

The captions to the bird illustrations indicate the bird's usual haunts, and if it is seen only in certain seasons, this fact is mentioned. Measurements indicate the size of the bird from the tip of the beak to the end of the tail. Notes to aid identification of the species are also included.

The mammals that are illustrated are accompanied by captions which indicate their average size. Those for hoofed mammals indicate their height at the shoulder. Others indicate the length of their bodies from nose to rump. The captions also give an indication as to when the animal is most active and therefore most easily observed.

The wild flowers are grouped according to their commonest colours; their most frequently used names are given in the captions, along with their habitats, the months in which they flower and their height or the length of creeping stems if they grow horizontally.

The illustrations of butterflies frequently show them on the plants they prefer to visit. The captions indicate the butterflies' usual habitats, the months when they are most frequently seen, and their wingspan.

Information about the sizes of the seashore animals are detailed in their captions, while the height of the trees is given on page 96. Selected identifying characteristics are given in the captions to the trees.

A hedgerow in early summer—one of the countryside's most rewarding habitats, since it shelters a wide variety of species. This illustration features some of the common, widespread plants and animals included in the following pages.

Birds

Canada Goose ▶
Fields and marshes near water; parks. Brown wings and body. Introduced from Canada. 95 cm.

Shag ▶
Rocky coats, where it nests in colonies. Has crest only in breeding season. Flies low, close to the water. 78 cm.

Cormorant ▶
Near the sea and some large inland waters. Has white thigh patch in breeding season. Larger than Shag. 92 cm.

Spring

◀ Mute Swan
Wide rivers, lakes, town parks. Not, as its name implies, mute. Britain's most common swan. 152 cm.

Mallard ▲
Inland waters and estuaries. Purplish-blue wing patch seen in flight. 58 cm.

▼ Wigeon
Near sea, especially in winter; lakes and marshes. Seen August-April; a few stay to breed. 46 cm.

◄ Pintail
Lakes and marshes, near coast in winter. Pointed tail and long, elegant neck. Seen September-March; a few stay to breed. 66 cm.

Shoveler ►
Quiet lakes and shallow water. Large, heavy bill. Pale blue forewings of both male and female show in flight. 51 cm.

▼ Teal
Inland waters and estuaries. The smallest duck in Britain. Dark bill. Quick and agile in flight. 35 cm.

▲ Tufted Duck
Lakes, ponds, gravel pits and parks. Dumpy, active diving duck. Note female's yellow eye. 43 cm.

▲ Shelduck
Coasts and estuaries, often in flocks; also large inland lakes. Female has no red knob on bill. 61 cm.

▼ Pochard
Lakes and backwaters. In flight, both sexes have dark wings with paler grey central bar. 46 cm.

▲ Red-breasted Merganser
Coastal areas; wooded lakes, rivers, in breeding season. 58 cm.

Grey Heron ▶
Near water: rivers, lakes and seashores. Head is drawn back in flight. 92 cm.

▲ Great Crested Grebe
Inland waters, sometimes on sea in winter. 48 cm.

▼ Little Grebe
Inland waters. Secretive and hard to spot. 27 cm.

Buzzard ▼

Often seen soaring over moors and farmland. Rare in east and south-east England. 54 cm.

▼ Kestrel

Moors, coasts, farmland; some nest in towns. Hovers when hunting. 34 cm.

Coot ►

Lakes, reservoirs, open water. Larger, heavier bird than Moorhen. 38 cm.

▲ Moorhen

Ponds, lakes and streams. 33 cm.

◄ Partridge

Farmland, moors. Small head, short tail and legs. Often in small groups. 30 cm.

▼ Pheasant

Farmland, scrub, woodland. Males can have white neckring. Male 87 cm, female 58 cm.

◄ **Redshank**
Seashores and wet meadows. Probes in mud. 28 cm.

▲ **Turnstone**
Shingle or rocky coasts. Turns over stones, seaweed, to find food. 23 cm.

▼ **Oystercatcher**
Seashores, estuaries. Often in groups. White band on throat in winter. 43 cm.

Common Sandpiper ▲
Rivers, streams and lakes. Seen April-October; a few in winter. 20 cm.

▼ **Ringed Plover**
Sandy and muddy shores. In summer, white wing bar shows in flight. 19 cm.

Lapwing ▲
Farmland, marshes, mudflats. 30 cm.

Curlew ▶
Mudflats and estuaries in winter; farmland, moors in breeding season. Rare in East Anglia and the South-East as a breeder. Britain's largest wader. 48-64 cm.

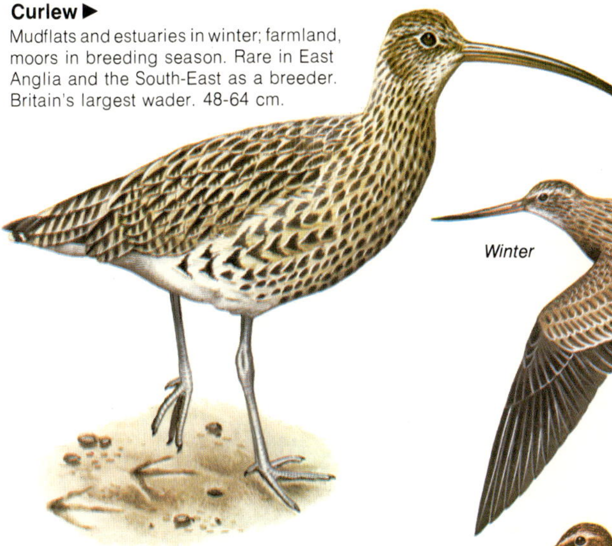

Winter

▲ Bar-tailed Godwit
Coastal mudflats and estuaries. Smaller than Black-tailed Godwit. 37 cm.

Black-tailed Godwit ▶
Coasts in winter; inland lakes, marshes in breeding season. White wing bar in summer. 41 cm.

Winter

◀ Whimbrel
Coastal mudflats and estuaries; meadows near the sea. 40 cm.

Woodcock ▼
Damp woods; not seen on shore. Secretive. 34 cm.

▲ Dunlin
Mudflats and estuaries. Common winter shorebird; less common in summer. 19 cm.

▲ Sanderling
Sandy shores along coasts. Seen August-May. Short, straight beak. 20 cm.

◀ Ruff
Marshes, wet meadows, edges of reservoirs. Seen mostly in spring and autumn. 29 cm.

Snipe ▼
Wet fields, marshes or lake edges. Probes while standing still. 27 cm.

Greenshank ▼
Coasts, marshes. Seen chiefly on migration. Some breed in Scotland. 30 cm.

▼ Knot
Sand or mudflats in estuaries. Larger than Dunlin. Seen mostly August-May. 25 cm.

▼ Common Tern
Near sea; also nests inland in Scotland. Seen April-October. 34 cm.

Summer

Summer

◀ Little Tern
Shingle beaches. Never has full black cap like other terns. Seen April-September. 24 cm.

Herring Gull ▼
Coastal ports and seaside towns. Wingtips are black with white spots. 56 cm.

◀ Black-headed Gull
Inland and near the sea. Dark brown "hood" in summer only. 37 cm.

Summer

Summer

Common Gull ▶
Coasts; often inland in winter. Smaller and less widespread than Herring Gull. 41 cm.

Lesser Black-backed Gull ▶
Coasts and inland. Mainly a summer visitor. 53 cm.

▼ Guillemot
Rocky coasts. Neck and throat are white in winter. Seen at cliff sites December-August. 42 cm.

◀ Fulmar
Rocky coasts. Nests on cliffs. Always sits, never stands. Mostly out at sea in winter. 47 cm.

Summer

Puffin ▶
Rocky islands and sea cliffs. Colourful bill in summer. 30 cm.

Summer

▼ Collared Dove
Large gardens, parks and farmland. Long white tail with black base. 30 cm.

◀ Stock Dove
Woods and cliffs; sometimes in towns. Darker, smaller bird than Woodpigeon. 33 cm.

Rock Dove ▼
Coasts, usually on sea cliffs. Town pigeons are descended from these birds. 33 cm.

Woodpigeon ▶
Farmland, woods and towns. White neck patch on adult. 41 cm.

▼ Short-eared Owl
Open country. Hunts in day-time or at dusk. 37 cm.

◀ Barn Owl
Open country, especially farmland. Mostly nocturnal. 34 cm.

Little Owl ▼
Farmland and wooded country. Underside is streaked. Often seen in daylight. 22 cm.

◀ Long-eared Owl
Edges of woods. Underside all dark. Nocturnal. 34 cm.

▲ Tawny Owl
Parks, woodland and farmland; sometimes towns. Large head. Nocturnal. 38 cm.

▼ Cuckoo
Anywhere in countryside. Male's song is well known. April-September. 30 cm.

◀ Kingfisher
Near rivers and lakes; seashore in winter. Dives from low perch or from a hover. 17 cm.

Swift ▶
Breeds mainly in towns; may fly over countryside. Seen end of April-August/September. 17 cm.

▼ Sand Martin
Banks and sandy cliffs. Seen April-September. 12 cm.

◀ House Martin
Suburban areas and countryside. Seen April-October. 13 cm.

◀ Swallow
Farms and open country; often near water. Seen April-September/October. 19 cm.

◀ Great Spotted Woodpecker
Woodlands. Large white patches on wings. 23 cm.

◀ Green Woodpecker
Deciduous woods, parks. Yellow-green rump seen in flight. Rare in Scotland. 32 cm.

Lesser Spotted Woodpecker ▶
Deciduous woods, parks. Not in Scotland. Sparrow-sized. 14 cm.

▲ **Meadow Pipit**
Upland moors and other open areas. Smaller, daintier than larks. 14.5 cm.

▼ **Dunnock**
Bushes and shrubs everywhere. Slender bill, unlike sparrows. 14.5 cm.

Tree Pipit ▲
Heaths and areas with scattered trees. Seen April-September. 15 cm.

▲ **Skylark**
Open country, especially farmland. Rises vertically to a great height in song flight. 18 cm.

♂

◄ **Yellow Wagtail**
Grassy places near water. Seen April-late September. 17 cm.

♂

Summer

◄ **Grey Wagtail**
By lochs or fast-flowing hill steams; waterfalls in lowlands. 18 cm.

▲ **Pied Wagtail**
Towns and countryside, usually near water. Females are greyer. Takes insects from the ground or the air. 18 cm.

▼ Willow Warbler
Gardens, woods and hedgerows. Flatter head and longer tail than Chiffchaff. Seen April-September. 11 cm.

▲ Sedge Warbler
Thick vegetation near water. Broad, pale stripe over eye. Seen April-September. 13 cm.

Wren ▶
Towns and countryside. Tiny, rotund bird with cocked tail. 9.5 cm.

Reed Warbler ▼
Reed beds. Not in Scotland. Seen April-September. 13 cm.

▲ Blackcap
Wooded areas. Seen April-September, a few in winter. 14 cm.

▼ Whitethroat
Thick, low bushes. Seen April-September. 14 cm.

▲ Garden Warbler
Hedges or woods with thick undergrowth. Seen April-September. 14 cm.

Chiffchaff ▼
Woods and copses. Seen March-September; a few in winter. 11 cm.

▲ Wood Warbler
Open woods with sparse undergrowth. Seen April-August. 13 cm.

♂

♀

Wheatear ▼
Open country, especially moors and downs. Seen March-October. 15 cm.

♂

▲ Whinchat
Rough grassland, moors with scrub, bracken, etc. Seen April-September. 13 cm.

♀

◀ Pied Flycatcher
Deciduous woods, especially oak. Seen April-September. 13 cm.

Spotted Flycatcher ▶
Parks, gardens, open woods. Seen May-September. 14 cm.

Blackbird ▼

In trees and bushes everywhere. Young are paler than female with breast more strongly spotted. 25 cm.

▼ Starling

Most places, including cities. In summer, has purple and green gloss and mostly yellow bill. 22 cm.

▲ Redwing

Farmland, commons and other open areas. A few breed in Scotland. Seen October-April. 21 cm.

◀ Fieldfare

Farmland, orchards, open areas. White underwings. Seen October-April. 25.5 cm.

▼ Redstart

Heaths, parks, open woods. Seen April-September. Rather Robin-like. 14 cm.

Robin ▲

Gardens, hedgerows and woodland. Juvenile is spotted, without any red. 14 cm.

◀ Song Thrush

Trees and bushes in towns and country. Smashes snails on stones. 23 cm.

Long-tailed Tit ▶

Hedgerows and woodland edges. 14 cm. (7.5 cm of which is the tail).

◀ Great Tit

Gardens and woodlands. Black band on chest. 14 cm.

◀ Blue Tit

Woods and gardens. Dark line on belly. 11 cm.

▲ Mistle Thrush

Woodland and open areas. Larger than Blackbird; paler, greyer than Song Thrush. 27 cm.

▼ Marsh Tit

Deciduous woods; infrequently in gardens. 11 cm.

▲ Coal Tit

Coniferous woods, parks, gardens. Oblong white patch on nape. 11 cm.

▼ Chaffinch

Farmland, hedgerows and woodland. Male is duller in winter. White wing bar seen in flght. 15 cm.

▲ Siskin

Usually coniferous woods in summer; birch, alder woods, sometimes gardens, in winter. 11 cm.

▲ Nuthatch

Deciduous wood and parks. Can descend trees head-first. Very short tail. Rare in Scotland. 14 cm.

▲ Hawfinch

Deciduous woodland, orchards. Very elusive. Big head and massive, broad bill. 16 cm.

◀ Treecreeper

Woodland, sometimes parks and gardens. Creeps up tree trunks using tail as support. 13 cm.

▲ Goldfinch
Open country, orchards and gardens. Distinctive broad yellow band across black wing. 12 cm.

▲ Bullfinch
Deciduous woodlands, hedges, orchards, gardens. Whitish wing bar on black wing. 15 cm.

◀ Linnet
Heathland and farmland. Forms large flocks in autumn on fields and waste ground. 13 cm.

▼ Lesser Redpoll
Coniferous and birch woods. Male has pink breast in spring. Streaked flanks (unlike Linnet). 12 cm.

▲ Greenfinch
Hedgerows, parks and gardens. Forages in flocks from autumn to spring. 15 cm.

▲ House Sparrow

Near houses in cities; on farms in the country. Distinctive black bib on male. 15 cm.

▼ Tree Sparrow

Farmland. White cheeks with black spot. Sometimes flocks with House Sparrow in winter. 14 cm.

▲ Corn Bunting

Open country, especially cornfields. Bigger than other buntings and finches. 18 cm.

▲ Yellowhammer

Farmland, heaths, young plantations. Flocks forage in fields in winter. Rare in Wales. 17 cm.

▲ Goldcrest

Large gardens and woods, especially conifers. Smallest British bird. 9 cm.

▲ Reed Bunting

Vegetation near water; may visit bird tables in winter. Male has less black on head in winter. 15 cm.

Carrion Crow ►

Open country, town, along coasts. Usually seen alone, in pairs or small groups. 47 cm.

▼ Jay

Woodlands, parks and gardens. White rump and blue wing flash show in flight. 32 cm.

◄ Magpie

Hedgerows, farmland, scrub. Large black and white bird. Long, slender tail. 46 cm.

▼ Jackdaw

Cliffs, farmland and towns. Small black and grey crow. Forms large flocks. 33 cm.

▲ Rook

Farmland, open copses, villages. Forms large flocks. Baggy thighs. Bare whitish face in adults. 46 cm.

Mammals

▼ Red Fox

Farmland and woods, sometimes mountains and towns. Mainly nocturnal. 65 cm.

▲ Badger

Woods, sometimes mountains. Nocturnal. Can stay underground for several days in cold weather without food. 80 cm.

▼ Roe Deer

Conifer plantations, especially near water. Mainly nocturnal; hides during day. 70 cm.

▲ Hedgehog

Hedgerows, ditches, parks, gardens and moorland. Mainly nocturnal. 25 cm.

▲ Mole

Underground in most kinds of soil in farmland, woods. Lives alone. Can swim well. 13 cm.

▼ Grey Squirrel
Woods, parks and gardens. Introduced from N. America. Diurnal. 27 cm.

Red Squirrel ▲
Mainly conifer woods. Partly replaced by Grey Squirrel in England. 23 cm.

▼ Rabbit
Farmland, woodland, sand dunes and hillsides. Active at dusk and dawn. 40 cm.

◀ Brown Hare
Open farmland and woodland. Mainly nocturnal, but can often be seen in day. 58 cm.

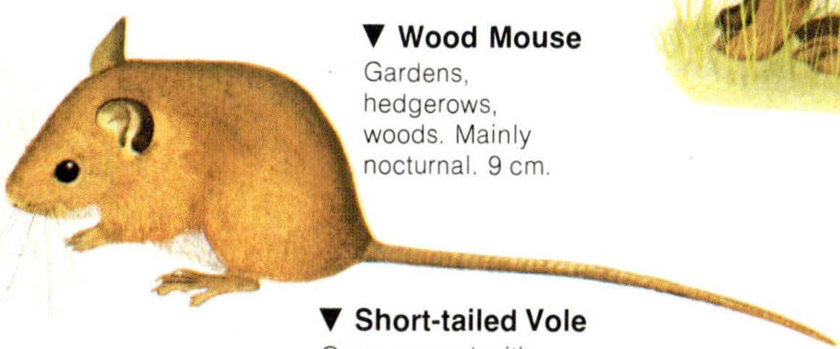

▼ Wood Mouse
Gardens, hedgerows, woods. Mainly nocturnal. 9 cm.

▼ Common Shrew
Rough pasture, woods, hedgerows, dunes and marshes. Active day and night. 7 cm.

▼ Short-tailed Vole
Open ground with rough grass. Most active at night; also seen in day. 11 cm.

◀ Grey Seal
Rocky shores, mainly along Atlantic coast; some on east coast of Scotland and north-east coast of Engıand. 3 m.

Common Seal ▶
Flat shores, estuaries and mudbanks on Scottish coasts and mainly east coast of England. Blunter head than Grey Seal. 1.5 m.

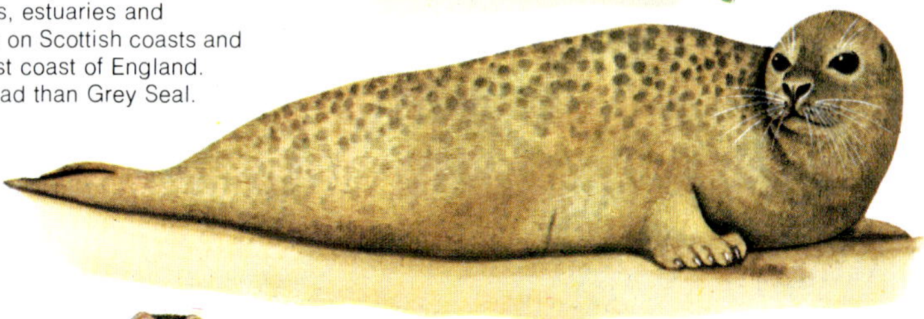

◀ Stoat
Woods, farmland, mountains. Tip of tail always black. Mainly nocturnal. 28 cm.

▲ Weasel
Same habitat as Stoat, but prefers dry places. Mainly nocturnal. 20 cm.

Water Vole ▶
Ponds, canals, streams and marshes. Mainly diurnal. May also be black. 19 cm.

Otter ▶
Alongside rivers, lakes; marshes, coasts and the sea. Nocturnal. More common in Scotland. 70 cm.

Wild Flowers

▼ Common St John's Wort

Damp, grassy places, open woods, hedgebanks. Less common in some northern areas. June-September. 30-90 cm.

▲ Lesser Celandine

Damp, shady woods, grassy banks and waysides. Creeping stems. March-May. 5-25 cm.

◀ Bulbous Buttercup

Dry, grassy places. Base of stem is swollen and bulb-like. March-June. 15-40 cm.

▼ Cowslip

Meadows, pastures, woods, copses. Absent from much of Scotland. April-May. 10-30 cm.

▼ Creeping Buttercup

Damp grassy places, woods, gardens. Long, leafy, creeping runners. May-August. Runners 15-60 cm.

▼ Creeping Jenny
Grassy, shady places; damp meadows, woods, under hedges. Rare in northern Scotland. June-August. Stems up to 60 cm.

◀ Yellow Rattle
Waysides and other grassy places. Seeds rattle inside ripe capsule. May-August. 12-40 cm.

Common Rockrose ▶
Grassy, rocky places. Not a rose. Leaves are hairy. May-September 5-30 cm.

Aaron's Rod ▶
Banks, waste places, open scrub. Rarer in Scotland. June-August. 30-200 cm.

◀ **Groundsel**
Waste places; a common garden weed. Flowers all year round. 8-45 cm.

▲ **Primrose**
Woods, hedges and fields. Rarer in the North. February-May. 8-15 cm.

◀ **Herb Bennet**
Woods, hedges, shady places. Fruits are hooked. June-August. 20-60 cm.

◀ **Broom**
Heaths, waste ground, open woods, scrubland. May-June. 60-200 cm.

▲ **Yellow Pimpernel**
Woods and shady hedgebanks. May-September. Trailing stems up to 40 cm long.

◀ Silverweed

Hedgebanks, grassy places. Creeping stems. May-August.

▲ Old Man's Beard

Woodland edges, hedgerows, scrub. Rare in Scotland and northern England. July-August. Up to 30 m.

Golden Rod ▶

Woods, cliffs, hedges. Rarer in the South-East. July-September. 5-75 cm.

▼ Bird's Foot Trefoil

Open, grassy places. Very long, creeping stems. Pods look like a bird's foot. May-June.

▼ Creeping Cinquefoil

Hedgebanks, grassy places. Creeping stems. May-August.

▲ Dandelion
Open grassy places and waste ground. March-October. 15-30 cm.

▼ Ragwort
Roadsides, waste ground, grassy places. Flowerheads in flat-topped clusters. June-October. 30-150 cm

Rape ▶
Roadsides and fields. May-August. Up to 1m.

▲ Wild Pansy
Grassy places and cornfields. Flowers can also be all yellow, all violet, or pink and white. April-September. 15-45 cm.

▼ Gorse
Heaths and commons. March-July. 60-200 cm.

▼ Viper's Bugloss

Waysides and sand dunes. Sharp hairs on stems. Bristly leaves. Rare in Scotland. June-September. 30-90 cm.

Common Forget-me-Not ▶

Roadsides, fields, and open grassy places. April-September. 15-30 cm.

◀ Sea Aster

Saltmarshes. Petals can also be white. July-October. 1 m.

◀ Common Speedwell

Grassy places and woods. May-August. 10-40 cm.

Common Milkwort ▶

Heaths, dunes, grassy places. May-September. 10-30 cm.

▼ Brooklime
In and by ponds, streams and other wet places. May-September. 20-60 cm.

Lesser Periwinkle ▶
Woods and hedgebanks. March-May. Flowering stems up to 15 cm.

Bugle ▶
Damp woods and grassy places. Has creeping runners. Leaves are often purplish. May-July. 10-30 cm.

Harebell ▼
Dry grasslands and heaths. Called Bluebell in Scotland. Locally common throughout Britain. July-August. 15-40 cm.

▲ Bluebell
Woods and hedgebanks. Flowers can also be white or pink. April-June. 20-50 cm.

▲ Honeysuckle

Climbing in woods, scrub and hedges. Fruits ripen to red in autumn. June-September. Up to 6 m.

▼ Greater Bindweed

Hedgerows, walls, waste places. Less common in the North. July-September. 1-3 m.

▲ Dog Rose

Hedges and woods. Flowers may be pink or white. Rarer in Scotland. June-July. 1-3 m.

▼ Bistort

Meadows and grassy roadsides, often near water. More common in northern England. June-August. 25-50 cm.

▼ Knotgrass
Waste ground, fields and seashores. A low, far-spreading plant. July-October. Creeping stems 3-200 cm.

Great Willowherb ►
Ditches, marshes, near streams. Rare in northern Scotland. July-August. 80-150 cm.

◄ Sea Bindweed
Sandy beaches; sometimes shingle. Rare in Scotland. June-August. Trailing stems up to 50 cm.

▼ Sand Spurrey
Sandy or gravelly places. Leaves end in a small bristle. May-September. 5-25 cm.

▲ Sea Milkwort
Grassy saltmarshes. Creeping stems. June-August. 10-30 cm tall.

◄ Thrift
Rocky cliffs near coast; mountains inland. March-October. 5-30 cm.

Common Centuary ▶

Grassland, dunes and woods. Rarer in Scotland. June-October. 2-50 cm.

◀ Heather or Ling

Heaths and moors. Flowers can also be white. Leaves overlap. July-September. Up to 60 cm.

▲ Rosebay Willowherb

Waste ground, roadsides. Seed has a hairy "parachute". July-September. 30-120 cm.

Bell Heather ▶

Dry heaths and moors. Not common in Midlands. July-September. Up to 60 cm.

▲ Herb Robert

Woods and hedgebanks. Fruit has a long "beak". May-September. 10-30 cm.

▼ Bilberry

Heaths, moors and woods. Blue-black berries. Flowers April-June. Up to 60 cm.

Ragged Robin ▲

Damp meadows, marshes, woods. Sepals form a tube. May-June. 30-75 cm.

Lady's Smock ▼

Damp meadows and near streams. Flower can be pink or white and lilac. April-June. 15-60 cm.

▲ Lesser Knapweed

Grassland and waysides. Stem is grooved below flowerhead. June-September. 15-60 cm.

◄ Hemp Agrimony
Damp places. Local to rare in Scotland. July-September. 30-120 cm.

▲ Policeman's Helmet
River banks, waste places, and near streams. Rare in some areas. July-October. 1-2 m.

Foxglove ►
Open woods, hedgerows, heaths. Poisonous. June-September. 50-150 cm.

▼ Valerian
Scrub, woods and grassy places. June-August. 20-150 cm.

◄ Red Campion
Woodlands and hedgerows. Rare in some areas. May-June. 30-90 cm.

◀ Watermint
Near water, marshes, damp woods. July-October. 15-90 cm.

Early Purple Orchid ▶
Woods and copses. Locally common throughout Britain. May-June. 15-60 cm.

◀ Wild Teasel
Roadsides, woodland edges, near streams. July-August. 50-200 cm.

◀ Devil's Bit Scabious
Wet grassy places. June-October. 15 -100 cm.

▲ Field Scabious
Dry grassland, waste places. June-September. 15-80 cm.

Common Dog Violet ▶
Hedgerows and woods. April-July. 5-20 cm.

Tufted Vetch ▼

Climbs on other plants in hedges and grassy places. June-August. Flowers 10 mm long.

▲ Ivy-leaved Toadflax

Old walls, occasionally rocks. Often forms clumps. May-September. Flowers 10 mm long.

Sea Lavender ▼

Muddy saltmarshes. Often forms large mats. Not in northern Scotland. July-October. 8-30 cm.

▲ Woody Nightshade

Hedges, woods, waste places. Poisonous. Not common in Scotland. June-September. Scrambling stems 30-200 cm.

▲ Scarlet Pimpernel

Cultivated and waste ground. A sub-species has small blue flowers. Rarer in Scotland. June-August. 6-30 cm.

◀ Field Poppy

Corn and other fields, waste ground. Rare in northern Scotland. June-August. 20-60 cm.

▼ Long-headed Poppy

Corn and other fields and waste ground. Longer capsule and paler petals than Field Poppy. June-July. 20-60 cm.

▼ Wood Woundwort

Woods, hedgebanks, waste ground. July-August. 30-100 cm.

◀ Greater Stitchwort
Woods, hedgerows and roadsides. Large petals are split to about half-way. April-June. 15-60 cm.

Wood Garlic ▼
Damp woods. Not common in northern Scotland. April-June. 10-25 cm.

▲ Wood Anemone
Woods. Often forms carpets. Flowers have up to nine petal-like sepals. March-May. 6-30 cm.

◀ Garlic Mustard
Hedges and woods. Not common in northern Scotland. April-June. 20-120 cm.

Dog's Mercury ▲
Woodlands. Not common in northern Scotland. February-April. 15-20 cm.

▼ White Bryony

Climbs in hedges and scrub. Berries are poisonous. Rarer in Scotland. May-September. Up to 4 m.

▼ Wild Strawberry

Woods and scrubland. Leaves have three leaflets. Can cover large patches. April-July.

Cow Parsley ▼

Hedgebanks, roadsides, ditches. Leaves are divided into feathery segments. April-June. 60-100 cm.

▼ Upright Hedge Parsley

Roadsides, grassy places. Flowers later than Cow Parsley, and leaves less feathery. July-August. 50-125 cm.

▼ Meadowsweet

Marshes, water meadows and near ditches. Flowers smell sweet. May-September 60-120 cm.

▲ Water Crowfoot

Ponds, streams and ditches. May-June. Flowers are 10-20 mm across.

Wild Carrot ►

Grassy places, especially near the sea. June-August. 30-100 cm.

Hogweed ▲

Open woods, roadsides, grassy places. June-September. 50-200 cm.

Daisy ▲

Short grassland, especially lawns. March-October. 3-12 cm.

▲ Nettle
Waysides, waste ground, woods. Has stinging hairs. June-August. 30-150 cm.

▼ White Dead Nettle
Roadsides, hedgerows and waste ground. Rare in north Scotland. May-December. 20-60 cm.

▲ Shepherd's Purse
Waysides and waste ground. Flowers all year. 3-40 cm.

▼ White Clover
Garden lawns, grassy places. June-September. Upright stems up to 25 cm.

◀ White Campion

Waysides, hedgebanks, waste ground. Sticky hairs. May-September. 30-100 cm.

◀ Bladder Campion

Roadsides and grassy places. Usually hairless. June-August. 25-90 cm.

◀ Sea Campion

Sea cliffs, shingle beaches. Smaller than Bladder Campion, with broader petals. June-August. 8-25 cm.

▼ Chickweed

Fields, waste places, gardens. Flowers all year. 5-40 cm.

▲ Corn Spurrey

Cornfields, cultivated land. June-August. 7-40 cm.

Yarrow ▲
Waste ground and grassy places. June-August. 8-45 cm.

▲ Ox-eye Daisy
Grassy places and roadsides. Upper leaves are toothed. June-August. 20-70 cm.

Sea Sandwort ►
Sand and shingle beaches. May-August. 5-25 cm.

▼ Pellitory-of-the-wall
Wall and rock crevices. Not in northern Scotland. June-October. 30-100 cm.

▲ Wood Sorrel
Woods and hedgebanks. Flowers close at night and in bad weather. Petals have lilac veins. April-May. 5-15 cm.

▲ Black Nightshade
Cultivated and waste ground. Rare in Scotland. July-September. Up to 60 cm.

▲ Bramble
Woods, scrubland, hedges, open ground. May-September. Arching stems up to 5 m.

▼ Greater Plantain
Cultivated land, waysides, lawns. Broad leaves. May-September. 10-15 cm.

▲ Ribwort Plantain
Grassy and waste places, lawns. Ribbed leaves. April-August. Up to 45 cm.

Butterflies

♀

Wall Brown ♂

▲ Wall Brown
Woodlands and rough, open ground. Often rests on walls. Not in northern Scotland. Seen March-September. 44-46 mm.

♂

Grayling ♀

▲ Grayling
Sandy places, chalk downs. Less common in Wales and East Anglia. Seen July-August. 56-61 mm.

♂

Meadow Brown ♀

▲ Meadow Brown
Meadows and other grassy places. Less common in Scotland. Seen June-September. 50-55 mm.

Small Heath ▶
Many areas including open woods, marshes and dry hillsides. Seen April-September. 33-35 mm.

Painted Lady ▶
Dry, open places. Likes thistles. Seen June-October. 62-65 mm.

Painted Lady

Red Admiral ▶
Gardens and woodland edges. Migrant from North Africa. Seen May-October. 66-68 mm.

▲ Small Tortoiseshell
Gardens and open places. Less widespread in Wales and Scotland. Seen April-November. 48-52 mm.
▼

Small Tortoiseshell

▲ Peacock
Gardens. Not present in northern Scotland. Seen August-October. 62-68 mm.

▲ Orange Tip

Woodland edges and hedgerows. Not in parts of Scotland. Seen April-June. 42-48 mm.

▼

Orange Tip

▲ Common Blue

Prefers downs and rough meadows. Seen April-September. 28-36 mm.

Common Blue

▼ Small Copper

All types of country. Less widespread in Scotland. Seen May-September. 26-30 mm.

Caterpillar of Small Copper

Large White

▲ Large White

Woods, gardens and open places. Caterpillar eats brassicas. Seen May-August. 62-64 mm.

Brimstone ♂

▲ Brimstone

Hedges, gardens and woodland paths. Adult hibernates. Not in Scotland. Seen June-September. 58-60 mm.

▼ Small White

Gardens and other cultivated places. Less widespread in Scotland. Seen May-August. 48-50 mm.

▼ Green-veined White

Open woodland and grassy places, gardens. Caterpillar eats leaves and seed-pods of Garlic Mustard. Seen May-September. 47-50 mm.

Seashore

◀ Gut Laver
A seaweed found in pools on upper and middle shores and estuaries. 20 cm long.

◀ Sea Lettuce
A seaweed found on middle and lower levels of rocky shores. 20 cm across.

Bladder Wrack ▲
A seaweed of rocky shores. Up to 60 cm long.

◀ Channelled Wrack
A seaweed found on rocks of the upper shore. 10 cm tall.

▼ Bread-crumb Sponge
On rocks, shells and seaweed holdfasts. 10 cm across.

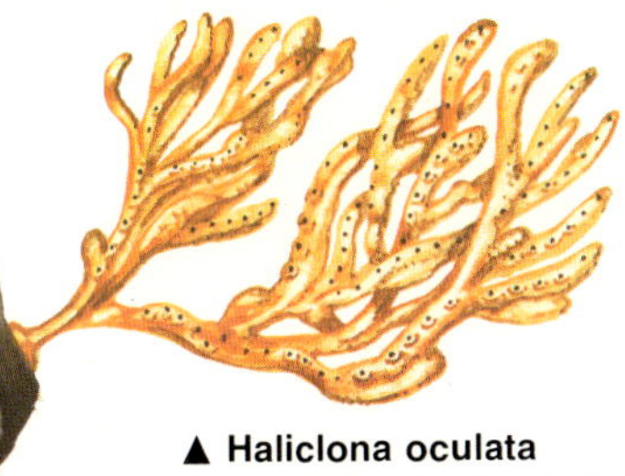

▲ Haliclona oculata
A sponge found on lower shores in fast currents and estuaries with muddy gravel. Up to 16 cm long.

Sea Oak ▶
A seaweed found in pools, on stalks of other seaweeds and on rocks. 20 cm tall.

▼ Beadlet Anemone
Rock pools at most levels of the shore. 5 cm high.

▼ Snakelocks Anemone
Rocky shores. Not on east or south-east coasts. Can be grey or greenish. 10 cm across.

▲ Daisy Anemone
In rock crevices or mud of shallow pools. 10 cm high.

Dahlia Anemone

▲ Dahlia Anemone
In crevices in rock pools. 15 cm high when open.

◄ Hermit Crab Anemone
On mollusc shells inhabited by Hermit Crab. 10 cm high.

◄ Common Hermit Crab
Mostly lower shore, in rock pools. 5-10 cm long.

▲ Common Limpet
On rocky shores, attached to rocks. 7 cm long.

▲ Common Periwinkle
On rocky and muddy shores. 2.5 cm high.

▲ Netted Dog Whelk
On mud and gravel off shore and on lower shore. 2.5 cm high.

▲ Saddle Oyster
On lower shore, attached to rocks. 6 cm wide.

▲ Common Whelk
Lower shore of rocky or sandy beaches. 8 cm high.

▲ Slipper Limpet
Low water and off shore, often attached to one another. 4-5 cm long.

▲ Common Mussel
Rocky shores, pier piles and estuaries. 1-10 cm long.

▲ Dog Whelk
On rocks and in crevices of lower shore. 3 cm high.

▲ Painted Topshell
On rocks and under stones on lower shore. 2.5 cm high.

▲ Common Oyster
Shallow and deep water. 10-15 cm long.

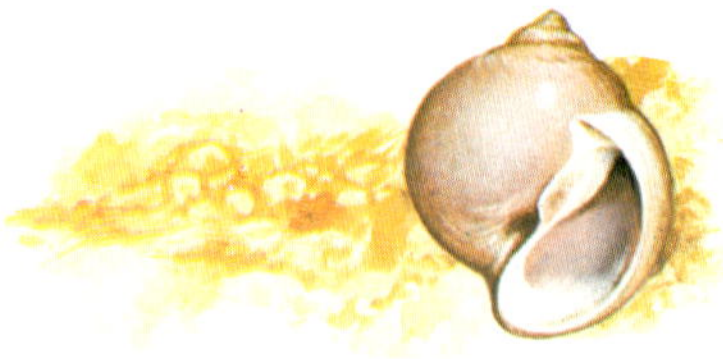

▲ Necklace Shell
Sandy shores. 3 cm high.

▲ Razor Shell
Burrows in mud. 12 cm long.

▲ Common Sand Gaper
Burrows in muddy sand on lower shore. 12 cm wide.

▲ Edible Cockle
In mud and sand of middle shore and below. 4 cm across.

▲ Rayed Trough Shell
Sand or gravel on lower shores. 5 cm long.

▲ Baltic Tellin
In mud and sand of seashores and estuaries. 2 cm long.

▲ Horse Mussel
From lower shore to deep water. 20 cm long.

▲ Flat Periwinkle
Under brown seaweed on rocky shores. 1 cm high.

▼ Brittle Stars
Under stones on lower shore. Small Brittle Star 3 cm across. Common Brittle Star 3-8 cm across.

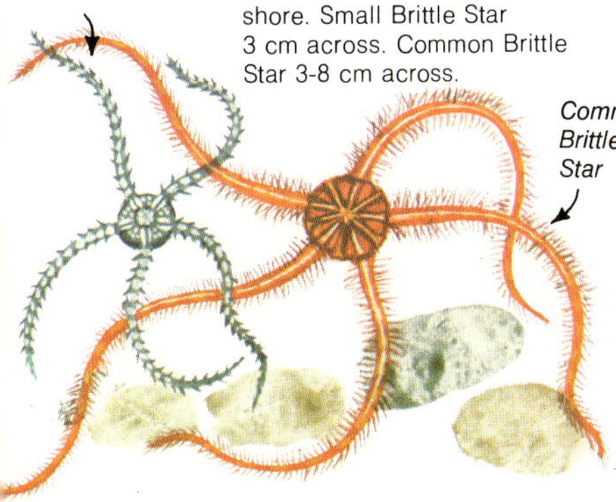

◀ Common Starfish
On the shore, 5-10 cm across; in deep water, up to 50 cm.

Sunstar ▼
In shallow water, lower shore. Up to 15 cm.

Sea Potato ▶
Burrows deep in sand of lower shore. 5-6 cm long.

▼ Edible Sea Urchin
Lower rocky shores and off shore. 15 cm across.

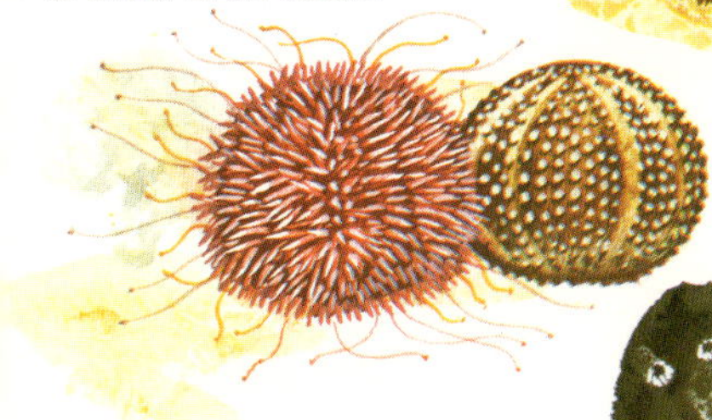

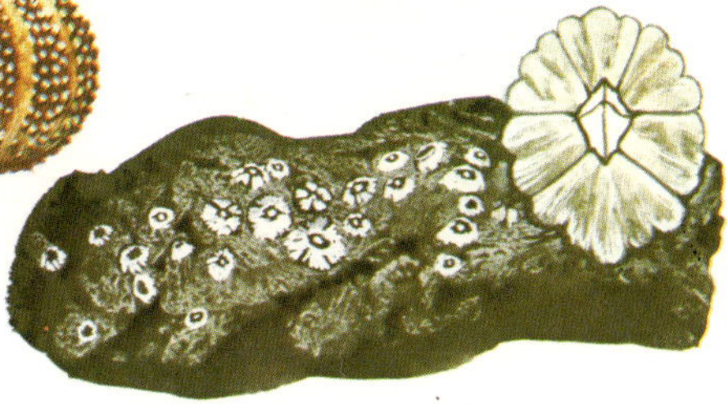

Acorn Barnacle ▶
On rocky shores. 5 mm long.

▼ Star Barnacle
On rocks of upper shore. 1 cm long.

▲ Moon Jellyfish
On all kinds of coasts. 15 cm across.

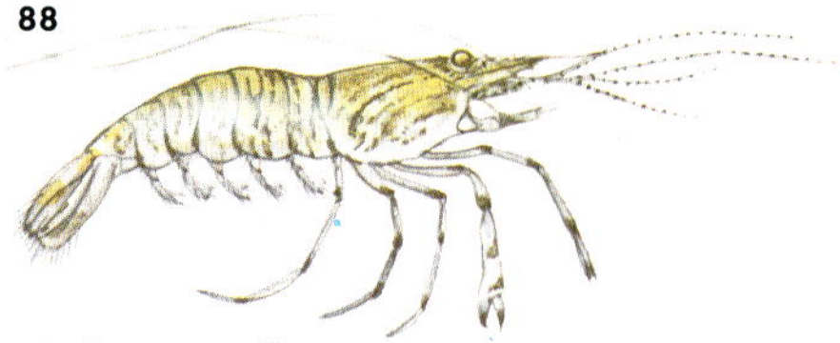

▲ Common Prawn
Shallow water and rock pools. 5-8 cm long.

▲ White Shrimp
Rock pools on lower shore; shallow waters of estuaries. 5 cm long.

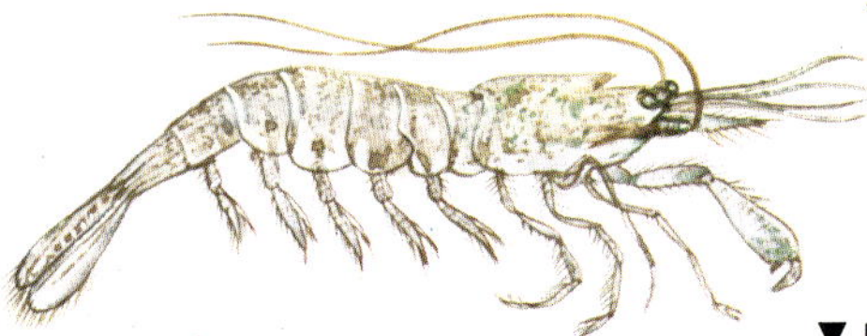

▲ Sand Shrimp
Sand estuaries. 5 cm long.

▲ Shore Crab
Sandy, muddy and rocky shores; estuaries. 8 cm across.

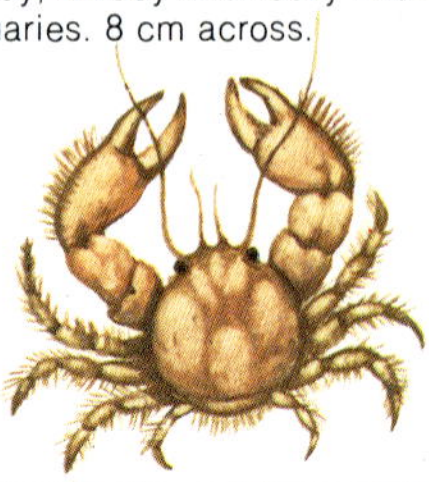

▲ Broad-clawed Porcelain Crab
Under stones on middle and lower shores. 1.2 cm across.

▼ Common Lobster
Only small ones in rock pools of lower shore. Can grow up to 45 cm long elsewhere.

▼ Montagu's Plated Lobster
Under seaweed and stones of lower shore. 4-6 cm long.

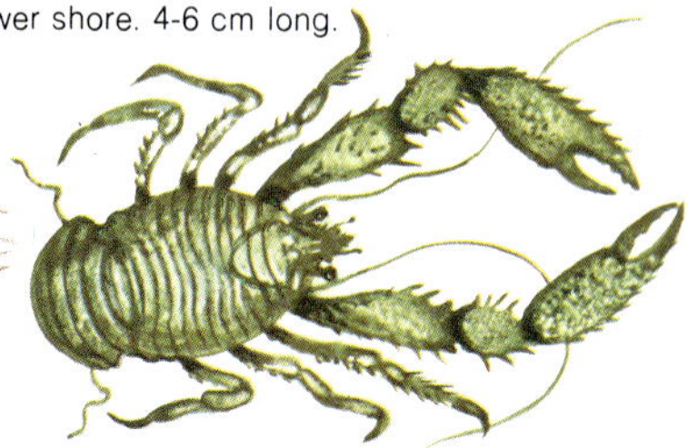

▼ Edible Crab
Only small ones in rock pools in lower shore. Can grow up to 11.5 cm long elsewhere.

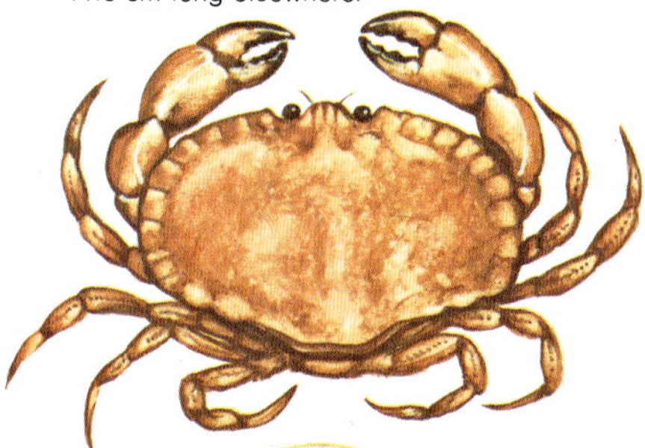

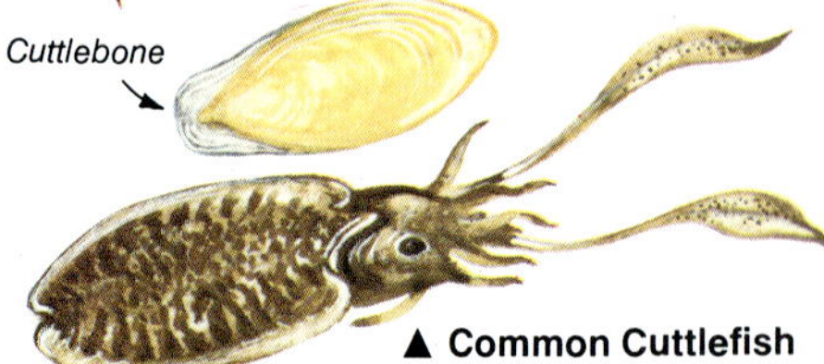

▲ Common Cuttlefish
In sheltered bays and washed up dead on strand line. 30 cm long.

Trees

▲ Scots Pine
Often in plantations. Needles are in pairs. Bark flakes off in "plates"

◀ Norway Spruce
Prickly needles. Small brown buds. Peg-like bumps left on twigs when needles are pulled off.

▲ Maritime Pine
Often in plantations. Rare in Scotland. Needles are in pairs. Long bud. Long, bare trunk.

▲ Sitka Spruce
Less common in eastern England. Prickly needles. Plump yellow buds. Yellow twigs.

▼ European Larch

Deciduous. Bunches of soft, light green needles leave small knobs on twigs when they fall.

▲ Douglas Fir

Soft, fragrant needles. Cones have three-pointed bracts on each scale.

▼ European Silver Fir

Rare in east and south-east England. Needles are green above, silvery below.

▲ Corsican Pine

Often in plantations. Needles are in pairs. Onion-shaped buds.

▲ Juniper
Needles are in threes with white band on upper surface. Berry-like cones.

▼ Yew
Often planted in churchyards. Leaves and berries are poisonous.

▲ Chile Pine
Also called Monkey Puzzle. Stiff, leathery leaves with sharp points.

▼ English Oak
Less common in northern Scotland. Acorns have long stalks. Leaves are short-stalked.

▼ Common Ash

Less common in northern Scotland. Seeds are in clusters called "keys".

▼ Rowan

Clusters of flowers appear in May. Berries ripen in August.

▲ Common Alder

Always found near water. Reddish catkins ripen to cone-like fruits.

▲ Sessile Oak

Acorn is usually stalkless. Leaves are long-stalked.

▼ Aspen

Often grows in thickets. Leaves tremble in the wind. White downy catkins appear in May on female trees.

▲ Goat Willow

Common on damp waste ground and in scrub woodland. Catkins, known as Pussy Willows, appear in late winter.

▼ White Willow

Common by water. Not in north-west Scotland. Weeping Willow is a variety of this species.

▲ Silver Birch

Catkins, known as "lamb's tails", are yellow with pollen in April. Bark peels off in ribbons.

▼ English Elm

Many have been killed by Dutch Elm disease. Clusters of red flowers appear before leaves.

▲ Sycamore

Paired, winged seeds twist as they fall. Bark becomes scaly.

▲ Common Lime

Yellowish-green flowers appear in July. Fruits hang from leafy wing.

▲ Common Beech

Leaves turn copper-brown in autumn. Nuts are triangular, encased in a husk.

▲ Horse Chestnut

Less common in Scotland. "Candles" of flowers (white or pink) appear in May.

▼ Sweet Chestnut

Flowers appear in June. Edible chestnuts are encased in a prickly fruit.

▲ Holly

Less common in northern Scotland. Evergreen. Berries found only on female trees.

▲ Common Hawthorn

Grows in thickets and hedgerows. Berries usually have only one stone.

The leaves and bark of each of the species shown below are illustrated on page 89–95.

Places to Visit

This section describes a selection of places to observe wildlife, ranging from nature reserves and good birdwatching areas to zoos, country parks, gardens and museums.

The descriptions of the places to visit are grouped by county and listed in alphabetical order. Each place has a number which is marked on an accompanying county map; long distance footpaths are also marked, but not numbered, and their descriptions are given directly below the maps.

The descriptions outline the main points of interest in each place. They also give details about location, points of access, and where relevant, telephone numbers and restrictions on opening times (opening times for some places, such as private gardens, can be irregular and are worth checking in advance). For some sites, nature trail leaflets and other publications are available for the visitor and this information is given together with the name and address of the organization from which they may be obtained. Where the name only is given, the address is listed under Useful Addresses on page 123.

In most cases the Ordnance Survey (1:50 000) sheet number and grid reference appear at the very end of the description (eg. OS 142: 205 890). The sheet number follows after "OS" and the grid reference after the colon. With large areas, such as forests and estuaries, the reference given is often for the best access points, or where these are too many to list, for the centre of the area. For some small gardens and museums, the reference occasionally indicates the nearest village.

In the case of nature reserves, reservoirs and privately-owned sites, the organization which owns, manages or leases them, is cited at the beginning of the description. In some, public access is restricted in order to protect the habitat and its wildlife, and a permit must be obtained in advance. This is indicated where applicable, together with details of where to apply for permission. Visitors to such places are reminded to take great care, and strictly adhere to any conditions and restrictions. In some areas, it may be possible to visit similar sites nearby, thus avoiding unnecessary pressure on reserves. (See also the Country Code and points on nature conservation on page 122.)

The English Tourist Board publishes a good range of literature on the region, and this is obtainable from the Regional Tourist Office (see page 123). Tourist Information Centres are found in many areas, particularly during the summer months, and these provide both literature and current opening times for local places of interest. Other useful addresses for organizations such as the naturalists' trusts, the Nature Conservancy Council and field centres, are also given on page 123.

Cornwall

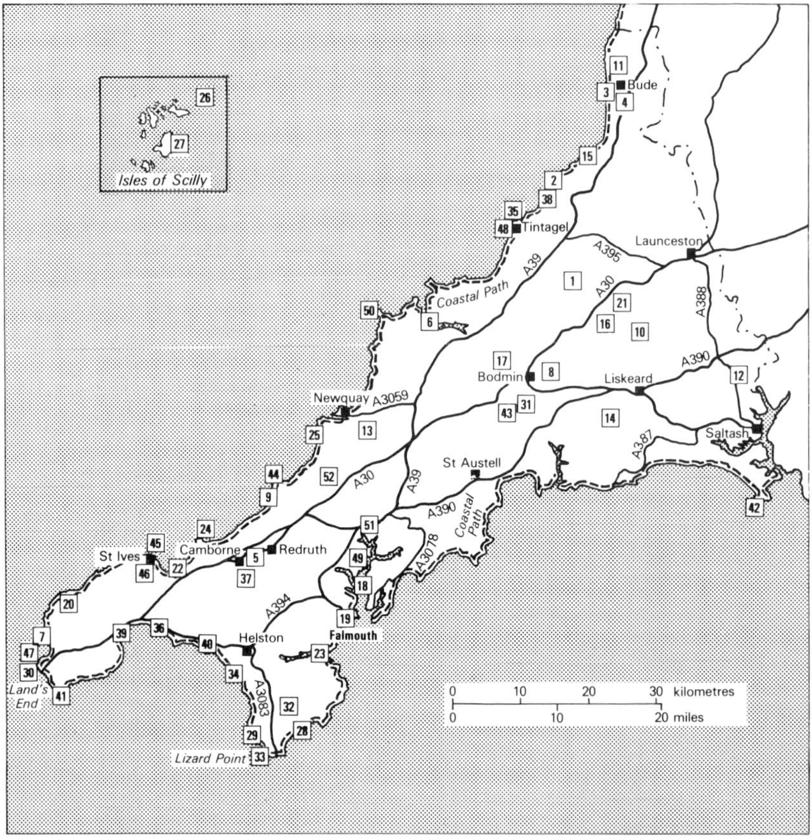

Cornwall Coast Path

This footpath is the central section of the South-West Peninsula Coast Path. It runs from Marsland Mouth in north Cornwall to Cremyll in the south. Much of it passes through the Cornwall Area of Outstanding Natural Beauty. Areas of particular interest along the route are described in the list of places to visit below.

☐Leaflet and guidebook about the path from the Countryside Commission. Walkers should take good maps with them. OS sheets 190, 200, 201, 203, and 204.

1 Bodmin Moor

Site of Special Scientific Interest. Extensive upland moor, including Rough Tor, a good example of typical tor scenery. Upland mosses and lichens can be seen around the tors and clitter slopes. Flowers include Pennywort and Eyebright; Sundew, Butterwort grow on the wetter moorland.

☐The moor starts 3½ miles/5 km west of Launceston; the A30 crosses it. Rough Tor, OS 200: 145 808.

2 Boscastle Harbour towards Widemouth Sands

National Trust. Site of Special Scientific Interest on the Cornwall Coast Path. Sea cliffs with large tracts of wind-pruned Oakwood and Gorse and Heather near the cliff edge. Also Heath Pearlwort, Wood Vetch and Royal Fern.

□Access to Boscastle Harbour off the B3266. OS 190: 095 915.

3 Bude Haven towards Coombe Valley
Steep sandstone cliffs where Natterer's and Daubenton's Bats roost in caves hollowed by the sea. Good walks along the cliff tops (part of the Cornwall Coast Path) or along the sandy beach at low tide.
□Access from Bude. OS 190: 200 069.

4 Bude Historical and Folk Exhibition
Exhibition of flora and fauna with reference to the history of the canal and harbour; also general exhibitions.
□Bude Stratton Town Council, The Castle, Bude (Tel: Bude 3576). Open daily in summer.

5 Camborne School of Mines
Good collection of local rocks, minerals and some fossils.
□Trevenson, Pool, Redruth (Tel: Redruth 714886). Open all year, Monday–Friday. North-east of Camborne on A30.

6 Camel Estuary
Large estuary on north coast; tidal marshes and sand dunes with Sea Meadow Grass, Sea Club Rush, Little Robin and Common Gromwell. Waders can be seen at most times of the year, and Pintail, White-fronted Goose, Divers and Grebes in winter; Grey Plover, Little Stint and Curlew Sandpiper in autumn. Grey Seal.
□6 miles/10 km north-west of Bodmin. OS 200. Good birdwatching points at:
a)Padstow
OS 200: 920 750.
b) Trebetherick Point
OS 200: 926 778.
c) Trewornan Bridge
OS 200: 987 744.

7 Cape Cornwall towards Clodgy Point
Stretch of coast on Cornwall Coast Path. Cliffs provide breeding sites for sea birds and Grey Seals. Coastal flora.
□Cape Cornwall is 5 miles/8 km north of Land's End. OS 203: 350 318.

8 Cardinham Woods
Forestry Commission. Coniferous plantations and small areas of coppiced Oak woodland. Nature trail starting at the car park and picnic place.
□Walkers using the Silvermine Trail should keep out of the fenced-off area, as it is dangerous. 2 miles/4 km east of Bodmin. Access off A38 onto unclassified road towards Cardinham. OS 200: 100 685.

9 Chapel Porth
National Trust. Areas of cliffs and heath. Nature trail along Chapel Porth valley over the cliff top, passing alongside a stream and old tin and copper mines. Typical heathland plants; also Betony, Prostrate Broom, Dyers's Greenweed, Madder, Golden and Common Samphire, Rock Spurrey, Spring Squill, and Adder's Tongue Fern. Basking Sharks and Grey Seals can be seen from the cliffs; Dragonflies and Damseflies are common. Butterflies include Common Blue, Grayling, Clouded Yellow, and Painted Lady. The shore is typical of the north Cornish coast with sandy inlets and rocky areas. Beware of venomous Lesser Weever Fish in the sand.
□Trail starts and finishes at the car park. 2 miles/3 km west of St Agnes village, north of Porthtowan. Access off B3277 road to St Agnes. OS 203: 698 496.

10 Cheesewring Quarry
Area of Bodmin Granite with Topaz, giving a peculiar rock formation which provides a rich marsh and bog vegetation. Acid-loving lichens coat the rock; birds include Wheatear and Wren.
□5 miles/8 km north of Liskeard. Access off B3254 at Upton Cross, then along unclassified roads. OS 201: 250 724.

11 Coombe Valley
Forestry Commission. Nature trail (managed by Cornwall Naturalists' Trust) through coppiced Oak and conifers.
□4 miles/6 km from Bude. Access off A39; turn west onto unclassified roads at Kilkhampton. OS 190: 225 115.

12 Cotehele
National Trust. Medieval house with terraced gardens leading down to sheltered valley, ponds and streams. Nature trail

through the woods beside the River Tamar.
☐Cotehele House, St Dominick (Tel: St Dominick 50434). House open April–December, Tuesday to Sunday; afternoons only. Garden open daily, all year. 8 miles/12 km south-west of Tavistock. Access of A390 onto unclassified road at Gunnislake. Gardens can also be approached by footpath from Calstock. OS 201: 423 685.

13 Dairyland and Country Life Museum
Modern dairy farm with museum showing living and working conditions of Cornish countrymen in the nineteenth century. Interesting local mineral collection.
☐Tresillion Barton, Summercourt, Newquay (Tel: Mitchell 246/7, 348/9). Open daily, April–October. South-east of Newquay, near Kestle Mill on A3058. OS 200: 858 594.

14 Deerpark Forest
Forestry Commission. Valley with mixed conifer and broadleaved trees: Oak, Beech, Ash, Willow, Red Oak, and Douglas Fir. Animals include Kingfisher, Badger, Fox, and Common Dormouse.
☐4½ miles/7 km south-west of Liskeard. Access off B3254 from Liskeard onto unclassified road to Herodsfoot. OS 201: 205 604.

15 Dizzard Point
National Trust. Dwarf Oakwood on exposed cliffs; also Birch, Rowan, Wild Service and Hazel trees. Shrubs include Spindle and Blackthorn. Ramsons, Lords and Ladies, Meadowsweet. Wild Strawberry and Sanicle can be seen here; also Cow-wheat and typical heathland flowers on more acid soil.
☐5½ miles/8 km south of Bude. Access off A39 north-west onto unclassified road to Dizzard at Wainhouse Corner. OS 190: 155 995.

16 Dozmary Pool
Large area of water surrounded by high moorland, with breeding Dunlin, Curlew, Stonechat, and Lapwing. Flowers include interesting Sedges, Water Starwort, Marsh Cinquefoil. Also a number of Dragonflies.
☐11 miles/17 km east of Bodmin. Access off A30 south onto unclassified road at Bolventor. OS 201: 193 746.

17 Dunmere Wood
Forestry Commission. Woodland on either side of the River Camel valley. Good area for fungi in autumn; Wild Daffodil and common Twayblade. Birds include Wheatear, Cuckoo, Redstart, and Carrion Crow. Also Fox and Stoat.
☐2 miles/3 km north-west of Bodmin on A389. OS 200: 045 683.

18 Fal Estuary
Site of Special Scientific Interest. Deep estuary with inter-tidal flats backed by a saltmarsh and tidal woodland of Alder, Willow and some mature Oak. (No public access to woodlands.) Flowering plants and ferns on the saltmarsh. Cormorants, Heron and Shelduck can be seen all the year, Black-tailed Godwit and Greenshank in winter, Green and Curlew Sandpipers in autumn. The best birdwatching places are in the sheltered areas of Devoran Creek, and the Rivers Tresillian, Truro and Fal.
☐OS sheet 204. Birdwatching points at:
a) Devoran to Penpoll
Access from Falmouth on A39 which runs along Devoran Creek north of Penryn. Turn east onto unclassified road to Devoran then follow coast to Penpoll.
OS 204: 800 390 to 814 390.
b) Ruan Lanihorne
Along River Fal; access off unclassified road running west-south-west from Tregony. OS 204: 895 420.
c) St Clement to Tresillian
Along River Tresillian; access from Truro on unclassified road south-west to St Clement, then by foot along river towards Tresillian. OS 204: 850 438.
d) Truro to Malpas
Along unclassified road south-east from Truro running along the river. Malpas, OS 204: 843 425.

19 Falmouth
Because of its mild climate, this south coast town has several interesting gardens with Mediterranean and sub-tropical trees and flowers.

□The following are open daily, all year:
a) Fox Rosehill Gardens
Melville Road.
b) Gyllyngdune Gardens
On the sea front.
c) Kimberley Park Gardens
Kimberley Park Road.

20 Geevor Tin Mining Museum
A museum with exhibits relating to the St Just tin-mining industry. Minerals from the Geevor Mine as well as a world-wide mineral display.
□Pendeen, St Just (Tel: St Just 788662). Open daily, April–October. North of St Just, off B3306. OS 203: 374 348.

21 Halvana Plantation
Forestry Commission. Coniferous forest with trail passing through old mining area of Bodmin Moor and leading to moorland. Leaflet from the Forestry Commission.
□Access off A30 between Bodmin and Launceston; turn south at Five Lanes village onto unclassified road signposted Tregirls. OS 201: 216 788.

22 Hayle Estuary
Mudflats with small area of saltmarsh attracting a large number of waders. Wintering birds include Black-throated and Great Northern Divers, Great Crested, Red-necked and Slavonian Grebes, Teal, Goldeneye, Red-breasted Merganser, Grey and Golden Plovers. Turnstone, Little Stint, Terns can be seen at other times of the year. Also Early Marsh Orchid, Portland Spurge, Hounds-tongue, Pyramidal Orchid, Yellow-wort, Cowslip and Sea Buckthorn. RSPB hide. Information from the site at Old Quay House Inn.
□5½ miles/8.5 km south-west of Camborne. Good birdwatching points along A30 at Hayle. OS 203: 550 380.

23 Helford Estuary
Stone-flanked and wooded sides to the estuary with the river flowing in a deep channel to the sea. Good examples of waders and marine animals.
□5½ miles/8.5 km south-west of Falmouth. OS sheets 203, 204. The following places in the area are of interest.
a) Cornish Seal Sanctuary
Sick, injured and orphaned seals can be seen in large pools, where they stay until they are able to return to the open sea.
□Gweek. Open daily, all year. At the head of the Helford Estuary. OS 203: 707 268.
b) Glendurgan Gardens
National Trust. Gardens, trees, shrubs; walled and water gardens; excellent views over the River Helford.
□Mawnan Smith, Falmouth. Open March–October, Monday, Wednesday, Friday. OS 204: 772 277.
c) Porth Navas
OS 204: 752 278.

24 Hell's Mouth to Godrevy Point
National Trust. Beautiful cliff coastline and heathland. Good for watching breeding sea birds, especially at Navax Point. Look for Guillemot, Puffin, Fulmar and Shag; also Raven and Buzzard. Grey Seals.
□North-west of Camborne. Access off B3301. Leave road on north side of Red River and follow path to Hell's Mouth. Navax Point. OS 203: 592 438.

25 Holywell Bay: Gull Rocks
Gull (or Carter's) Rocks are just off Penhale Point in Holywell Bay. Site of a well-known auk colony, with large numbers of Guillemot, Razorbill and Puffin.
□4½ miles/7 km south-west of Newquay. Access off A3075 onto unclassified road to Holywell; walk out to Penhale Point. OS 200: 755 595.

26 Isles of Scilly
Series of bevelled granite masses separated by shallow seas. Rich flora and fauna, including Sea Beet, Bittersweet and Sea Pearlwort on rocky shores; Prickly Saltwort, Yellow Horned Poppy on the sands; Buckshorn Plantain, Portland Spurge and Viper's Bugloss on the dunes. Plants to be seen in pools and mud include Sea Spurrey, Crowfoot, Starwort, Marsh Pennywort, Bog Pimpernel, Lesser Spearwort, Water Purslane, Lesser Water Plantain, Marsh Bedstraw, Marsh Cudweed, Royal Fern, Yellow Flag, Gipsywort, and Great Reedmace. Good selection of birds such as Puffin, Guillemot, Razorbill, Storm Petrel, Kittiwake, Fulmar, Common Sand-

piper, Golden Oriole, and Firecrest; also rare visitors – Northern Waterthrush, Bobolink and Hoopoe. There are two nature trails on the main island, St Mary's.
□Access restrictions on the uninhabited islands at different times of year. Contact General Manager (Tresco), Estate Office, Isles of Scilly (Tel: Scillonia 22849). St Mary's can be reached by boat, air or helicopter from Penzance. Also regular inter-island launches from St Mary's. OS sheet 203.

27 Isles of Scilly Museum
Some local geology and exhibits of birds, moths, butterflies, and shells, as well as fresh summer flowers from the islands.
□St Mary's (Tel: Scillonia 22337). Open daily in summer except Sunday.

28 Kennack Sands
Two wooded valleys lead down to the sandy bays which are backed by rocky cliffs. Stonechat and Buzzard; Anemones and Painted Topshells on the shore.
□2 miles/3 km from the Lizard. Access off B3293, south onto unclassified road at Traboe Cross. OS 204: 734 165.

29 Kynance Cove
Cornwall Naturalists' Trust/National Trust; Site of Special Scientific Interest. Multi-coloured Serpentine cliff line, split up by sandy bays and caves. Fantastic rock formations, but explorations can be dangerous. Hairy Violet and Knotted Bur Parsley on base-rich soils; Butcher's Broom and Bloody Cranesbill on sand. Unique heathland flora, also Wild Asparagus and Juniper.
□2 miles/3 km north-west of the Lizard. Access off A3083 via toll road. OS 203: 685 133.

30 Land's End
Exposed area of granite cliffs with a good example of splash zone vegetation. Flowers include Rock Samphire, Sea Plantain, Buckshorn Plantain, Rock Sea Lavender, Rock Sea Spurrey, Sea Carrot and Sea Pink. Colourful coastal lichens.
□9 miles/14 km south-west of Penzance. At the end of A30. OS 203: 343 251.

31 Lanhydrock
National Trust. Park and mixed woodland on both sides of the River Fowey. Fine shrubs and formal gardens. Nature trail through the woods where Redstarts and Pied Flycatchers can be seen; also Silver-washed Fritillary.
□(Tel: Bodmin 3320). Gardens open daily, all year. 2½ miles/3 km south-east of Bodmin on B3268. OS 200: 085 636.

32 The Lizard National Nature Reserve
Nature Conservancy Council. Heathland at Goonhilly Downs, in the central part of the Lizard. The mild oceanic climate together with the geology and southerly location has given rise to two types of heathland: "tall heath" with Cornish Heath, Purple Moor Grass and Black Bog-rush, and "short heath" characterized by short, stunted growths of Western Gorse, Purple Moor-grass, Ling, Bell Heather and Cross-leaved Heath. The wetter areas have a rich cover of mosses, liverworts and lichens as well as Pillwort, Yellow Bartsia, and Water Crowfoot. Nearer the coast, Large Lizard Clover, Sand Quillwort and Ciliate Rupturewort occur.
□Much of the Lizard heaths is privately owned and the owners' permission is required before entering these areas. For permits and information about the reserve, contact the Nature Conservancy Council, Roughmoor, Bishop's Hull, Taunton, Somerset. The Goonhilly Downs are east of the A3083 Helston-Lizard roads and south of the B3293. OS 204: 730 190.

33 Lizard Point
Site of Special Scientific Interest; heathland on schist, above an exposed rocky shore with Brittle Stars and various seaweeds on the shore; Fuchsia and Lesser Butterfly Orchid in the hedges and fields; also common fungi. Wildlife includes Hare, Adder and Common Lizard, and coastal birds.
□Just south of Lizard village. OS 203: 695 115.

34 Loe Pool and Bar
National Trust. Large freshwater lake separated from the sea by a shingle bank.

Marshy, reedy area with fringing woods. Good place to see wintering ducks: Teal, Wigeon, Shoveler, Tufted Duck, Gadwall and Goldeneye. Flowers include White and Yellow Water-lilies, Marsh Marigold, Butterbur, and on the sand dunes Sea Campion, Sea Bindweed, Yarrow, and Bird's Foot Trefoil.
□About 1 mile/2 km south-west of Helston. Access off B3304 to Porthleven; walk through Penrose Estates. OS 203: 642 241.

35 Lye Rock
Largest Puffinry in Cornwall; Razorbill and Guillemot breed here in summer.
□Just north-east of Tintagel. Access off B3263 at Bossiney. OS 200: 064 899.

36 Marazion Marsh
A fresh marsh with reed beds and shallow pools. St Michael's Mount (National Trust) is across the causeway. An important birdwatching area; waders on passage in spring and autumn. Large numbers of divers and Grebes in winter. Marine animals include sponges, molluscs, Cornish Sucker Fish, and Blennies.
□3½ miles/5 km east of Penzance. Access off A394. OS 203: 516 306.

37 Pendarves Wood
Cornwall Naturalists' Trust educational nature reserve. Deciduous woodland and conifers; small lake.
□Restricted access. Contact Administration Officer, Trendrine, Zennor, St Ives, Cornwall (Tel: St Ives 6926). Off B3303, 1½ miles/2.5 km south of Camborne. OS 203: 645 382.

38 Peter's Wood
Cornwall Naturalists' Trust/National Trust. Mainly Sessile Oak with Downy Rose, Tunbridge Filmy Fern and Polypody Fern. Razorbills breed here; numerous Badgers; Grey Seals offshore.
□Near Boscastle or 3 miles/5 km east of Tintagel on the B3263. OS 190: 098 915.

39 Penzance
Rural town fringed with woodlands and farming land. Look for Toothed Medick, Fragrant Agrimony, and Small Cudweed in open places and Cornish Moneywort in woods.
□OS sheet 203. The following sites in the town are of interest:
a) Geological Museum
Good collection of Cornish rocks, minerals and fossils.
□Alverton Street. Open May–September, Monday–Friday afternoon.
b) Penlee House Museum
Exhibition of local natural history.
□Penlee Park (Tel: Penzance 3625). Open every afternoon except Sunday.
c) Trengwainton Garden
National Trust. Walled garden with Rhododendrons and Magnolias; also fascinating stream flora.
□Open March–October, Wednesday to Saturday. 2 miles/3 km north-west of Penzance off B3312. OS 203: 445 315.

40 Praa Sands
Sandy beach backed by a small dune system. Flowers include Yellow Bartsia, Butcher's Broom, Small Cudweed, Prostrate Toadflax, Common and Golden Melilot.
□5 miles/8 km west of Helston. Access off A394, turning south just after Ashton onto unclassified road. OS 203: 580 280.

41 Porthgwarra Valley
The valley cuts into an impressive cliff coastline. Flora and fauna typical of the Cornish cliffs. Good selection of butterflies and moths; Common Blue, Small Copper, Green Hairstreak, Red Admiral, Burnet Moth, Drinker Moth, Oak Eggar and Emperor Moth. Whales, Seals, Porpoises and Dolphins can be seen out at sea; also Mako, Porbeagle and Common Blue sharks.
□4 miles/6 km south-east of Land's End. Access off B3315 south onto unclassified road at Polgigga. OS 203: 372 218.

42 Rame Head
Headland at Whitsand Bay, south of the Tamar Estuary. Impressive cliff walk. Good selection of coastal flowers as well as Burrowing Clover and Shore Dock. Birds include Buzzard, Sparrowhawk, Oystercatcher, and Rock Pipit. Also Fox, Stoat

and Weasel.

□Access off A374 at Antony onto B3247 towards Millbrook; after 4½ miles/7 km turn south onto unclassified road to Rame. OS 201: 418 483.

43 Redmoor

Cornwall, Naturalists' Trust nature reseve. Typical mid-Cornish moor (once mined for tin) with wide range of habitats: dry and wet heath, marsh and open water. Willow and Alder provide cover for a wide selection of birds and insects.

□Restricted access. Contact Administration Officer, Tendrine, Zennor, St Ives, Cornwall (Tel: St Ives 6926). 6 miles/9 km south of Bodmin on B3268. OS 200: 080 612.

44 St Agnes Head

Headland with rich heathland flora; extremely good area for birdwatching. Breeding birds include Kittiwake, Fulmar, Black-headed Gull, Raven, Razorbill, Guillemot, Yellowhammer, and Chiffchaff. Look for Sabine's Gull, Storm Petrel and Arctic Skua. The Common Lizard and Adder can sometimes be seen; also Common Blue, Clouded Yellow and Painted Lady butterflies.

□4½ miles/7 km south-west of Perranporth. Access off B3285 onto unclassified road at St Agnes. OS 203 or 204: 698 516.

45 St Ives Island or St Ives Head

Good place to watch for sea birds on passage, particularly after north-westerly winds in autumn when birds are blown off course. American Sabine's Gulls are annual visitors, also Leach's Petrel and Storm Petrel, often with Manx and Sooty Shearwaters amongst them.

□Just north of St Ives. OS 203: 520 413.

46 St Ives Museum

Some local fauna and geology.

□Wheal Dream, St Ives (Tel: St Ives 796005). Open daily in summer except Sunday morning.

47 Sennen Cove

Granite cliffs, sand beach and dunes, with vistas of the inland moor. Flowers include Sand Spurrey, Common Poppy, Rough Chervil, Knotted Bur Parsley, and Lesser Water Plantain. Breeding birds are Kittiwake, Greater Black-backed Gull and Shag.

□Off A30 1½ miles/2.5 km from Land's End. OS 203: 353 264.

48 Tintagel Head and Cliffs.

National Trust. Rock promontories with steep inclines and massive caves. Good views from the cliffs of Puffin, Razorbill, Shag and Cormorant.

□4 miles/6 km south of Boscastle. Access off B3263 beyond Tintagel. OS 200: 048 889.

49 Trelissick

National Trust. In spring these gardens are ablaze with Rhododendrons, Azaleas. Nature trail runs alongside the River Fal.

□Feock, Truro (Tel: Devoran 862090). Open March–October, daily. Access off A39 from Truro; turn south-east after 2 miles/3 km onto B3289 for a further 2 miles. OS 204: 837 396.

50 Trevose Head and Constantine Bay

Dramatic headland formed by volcanic greenstone sill. Blue Fleabane, Saltwort, Ploughman's Spikenard on sandy terrain; Rest-harrow on the rockier parts and Early Purple Orchid in damp places.

□10 miles/16 km north-east of Newquay. Access off B3276. OS 200: 849 766.

51 Truro County Museum

An excellent mineral collection and displays of Cornish plants and birds.

□River Street (Tel: Truro 2205). Open daily except Sundays.

52 Ventongimps Moor

Cornwall Naturalists' Trust nature reserve. Heath and bogland on peat and clay giving a mixed habitat of dry and wet heath with some bog; Willow and Alder carr. Interesting selection of insects.

□Restricted access. Contact Administration Officer, Tendrine, Zennor, St Ives, Cornwall (Tel: St Ives 6926). 4 miles/6 km south-east of Perranporth. Access off A3075. OS 204: 780 513.

Devon

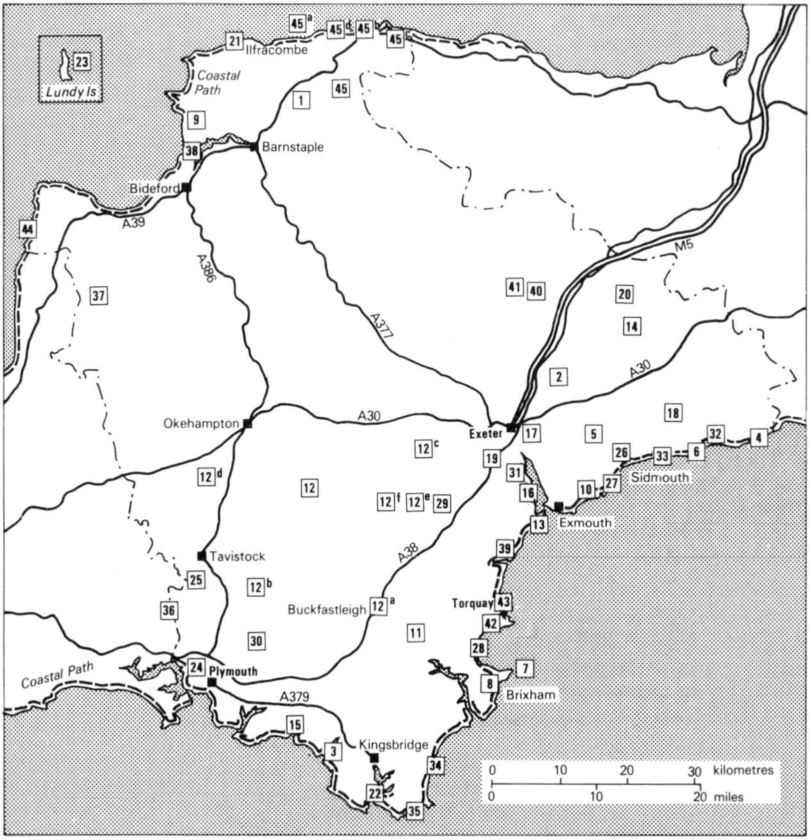

Somerset and North Devon Coast Path
See entry under Somerset for details of this long distance path. Areas of particular interest along the route in North Devon are described in the list of places to visit below.

South Devon Coast Path
This part of the South-West Peninsula Coast Path runs from Plymouth to Lyme Regis. Most of it passes through South Devon and East Devon Areas of Outstanding Natural Beauty. Areas of particular interest along the route are described in the list of places to visit below.
□Leaflet describing the path from the Countryside Commission. A guidebook published annually and with accommodation details is available from the South West Way Association, c/o Mrs D. Y. Lancey, "Kynance", Old Newton Road, Kingskerswell, Newton Abbot. Walkers should take good maps. The route is well marked on OS sheets 192, 193, 201 and 202.

1 Arlington Court
National Trust. Nature reserve with parkland, hanging woods, lakes, river and ponds. Heronry and Wildfowl Refuge; Red Deer; nature trail. Park is grazed by Shetland Ponies and Jacob Sheep.
□(Tel: Shirwell 296). Open daily, April–October. 5 miles/8 km north-east of Barnstaple on A39. OS 180: 611 405.

2 Ashclyst Forest
600 acres/243 ha of woodlands on clay soils. Oak, Chestnut, Ash, with newly planted blocks of conifers. Rich flora and fauna. Birds include Nuthatch, Treecreeper, Woodpeckers, Sparrowhawk, and Tawny Owl. Fallow and Roe Deer. Look for White Admirals on Bramble.
□6 miles/10 km north-east of Exeter. Access off B3183; turn east just past Broadclyst onto unclassified road. OS 192: 000 990.

3 Avon Estuary
Mud and sand estuary; good Oak coppice woodland on the steep sides. Redshank, Curlew, Whimbrel, Oystercatcher, Dunlin, Sanderling, and occasionally Greenshank, from July to April; Shelduck in summer. Heronry near Bantham. Look for Sea Aster on the saltmarshes.
□3 miles/5 km west of Kingsbridge. Tidal head at A379 crossing; take low-water road down west side for best views of waders on the mud. Access to mouth from Bigbury-on-Sea or Bantham; both signposted from A379. OS 202: 670 440.

4 Axmouth–Lyme Regis Landslip National Nature Reserve
Nature Conservancy Council. Area of Outstanding Natural Beauty. Very dense Ashwood on the landslip terraces with typical woodland birds. Flowers include Clematis, Crow Garlic and orchids.
□Permit required for visitors leaving the footpath. Contact the Nature Conservancy Council Regional Office, Roughmoor, Bishop's Hall, Taunton, Somerset. 24 miles/38 km east of Exeter on A3052. For Axmouth, take B3172 off main road 8 miles/13 km beyond Sidford; for Lyme Regis, stay on A3052. OS 193: 270 890.

5 Aylesbeare and Harpford Commons
RSPB nature reserve and Site of Special Scientific Interest. Dry and wet heath with scattered Scots Pines. Typical heathland flowers and butterflies. Birds include Stonechat, Tree Pipit, Nightjar, Buzzard, and Sparrowhawk.
□Unrestricted access but keep to the footpaths. 6 miles/10 km east of Exeter off A3052. Car park ½ mile/1 km east of Halfway Inn. OS 192: 055 910.

6 Beer
Site of Special Scientific Interest. Good exposures of chalk in cliffs, on either side of the small bay. Cliff top south-west of village is a good site for watching seabirds, especially gulls, Gannet and Fulmar. Look for Warblers, Chats and Redstarts during autumn migration. Cliff-top flowers include Carline Thistle, Salad Burnet, Stinking Hellebore, Stinking Iris, Mullein, Harebell, Dogwood, Clematis, and orchids. Coastal footpath.
□22 miles/35 km east of Exeter. Access off A3052 5 miles/8 km east of Sidford; turn south onto B3174 at Bovey Down. OS 192: 230 895.

7 Berry Head Country Park
Local Nature Reserve; Site of Special Scientific Interest. 200 ft/60 m high limestone cliffs with very level, plateau-like top. Limestone turf with typical flowers, richer flora on south-facing cliff top. Nature trail. Stonechat, Linnet and Wren breed on the cliff top and many small birds pause on migration. Guillemot, Kittiwake, Fulmar, Cormorant, Shag, gulls, and Jackdaw breed on narrow cliff ledges. Kestrels also breed in the area and Peregrine Falcons are sometimes seen during spring and autumn migration. Flowers include Thyme, Salad Burnet, Rockroses (including White Rockrose), Kidney Vetch, Bird's Foot Trefoil, Sea Carrot, and some orchids. April–July is the best time to visit. Trail leaflet available on site.
□South end of Torbay; access through Brixham. Berry Head is signposted from the town centre. OS 202: 940 560.

8 Brixham Museum
Local natural history, particular of Berry Head. Flora, geology and seashells.
□Bolton Cross, Brixham (Tel: Brixham 4207). Open daily in summer.

9 Braunton Burrows National Nature Reserve
Nature Conservancy Council. Nature reserve covers 1492 acres/604 ha part of

which is occasionally closed for use by the Ministry of Defence. It is the largest system of sand dunes in the South-West. The dunes reach 100 ft/30 m in height in some areas and there are pools in slacks. Shelduck, Wheatear, Stonechat, Linnet, and Goldfinch breed in the area; Merlin, Harrier and Short-eared Owl hunt the dunes during migration. Good selection of flowers on the dunes, such as Sea Rocket, Saltwort, Portland Spurge, Sand Sedge, Sea Storksbill, and Lesser Hawkbit; also mosses and liverworts. Shoreweed, Sea Rush, Water Germander, Club-rushes, Sea Pearlwort, Creeping Willow, and Marsh Helleborine grow in the dune slacks. Seaside Pansy and Hairy Violet flower in early summer. Rabbits and foxes can be seen; also snails, lizards and grasshoppers. Small Tortoiseshell, Peacock, Painted Lady, Common Blue, and Fritillaries fly in summer; Burnets and Cinnabar Moths breed in large numbers. Behind the dunes is Braunton Great Field, a medieval common field divided into strips and still in different ownerships.

□Visitors are warned to keep clear when red flags are flying; this indicates military exercises are in progress. Military use is also advertised in local papers and at police stations. Sites signposted as Danger Areas should be avoided at all times. Warden's address: Broadeford Farm, Heddon Mill, Braunton (Tel: Braunton 812552). 8 miles/12 km north-west of Barnstaple. Access off A361 at Braunton onto B3231. OS 180: 450 350.

10 Budleigh Salterton Museum

Good local museum with geological and natural history exhibits.

□Budleigh Salterton (Tel: Budleigh Salterton 2666). Open daily, July–August; afternoons only from Easter–June, September–October, Christmas period–January.

11 Dartington Hall Gardens and Estate

Gardens with mature Oak, Beech, Chestnut and Pine. Estate has many small copses and one large plantation; nature and farm trails. There is also a riverside walk along the River Dart. Typical garden flowers and birds such as Treecreeper, Nuthatch, Spotted Flycatcher, Blackcap; Kingfisher on the River Dart; Buzzard and Raven on the estate.

□(Tel: Totnes 863291). Open daily, all year. 1 mile/2 km north-west of Totnes on Buckfastleigh Road. OS 202: 798 628.

12 Dartmoor National Park

A detailed description of the park is given on pages 18–20. Leaflets and information available from National Park Information Centres at Bovey Tracey, Princetown, Tavistock, Newbridge, Steps Bridge, and Postbridge.

□OS sheets 191, 201 and 202. The following places in the park are of particular interest:

a) Buckfastleigh Caves

Devon Trust for Nature Conservation nature reserve. Site of Special Scientific Interest. Caves have Pleistocene mammal fossils, from inter-glacial (tropical) times, and bat colonies. Limestone quarries with scrub; some wet fen. Museum has interesting displays relevant to the area.

□The caves may be entered only with a guide; times of opening advertised by the Dartmoor National Park Authority and the Pengelley Cave Research Trust. Museum is open at the same time as the caves. Leave A38 at Dart Bridge, follow signposts to Buckfastleigh. OS 202: 740 663.

b) Burrator Reservoir and Forest

South-West Water Authority. Good waymarked walks through forest and up onto surrounding tors; Sheepstor and Leather Tors give spectacular views.

□Access to water's edge by permit from South West Water Authority, 3-5 Barnfield Road, Exeter. 9 miles/14 km north-east of Plymouth on A326. Access off B3212, then onto unclassified road 2 miles/3 km from Yelverton. OS 202: 555 685.

c) Dunsford to Fingle Bridge

Oak coppice and coniferous plantations in the River Teign valley with nature trails, wood and riverside walks. Teign Valley Woods is a property of the National Trust; Dunsford Nature Reserve is managed by the Devon Trust for Nature Conservation. Rich woodland bird population; good Salmon and Sea Trout in the river. The nature reserve has fine displays of Wild Daffodils in spring; leaflet available on the site in March and April, and from the Devon Trust for Nature Conservation.

□7 miles/11 km west of Exeter on B3212. Can be explored on valley bottom paths from Steps Bridge (B3212), Clifford Bridge (via Dunsford) and Fingle Bridge (via Drewsteignton, off old A30). Steps Bridge, OS 191: 805 883; Fingle Bridge OS 191: 743 900.

d) Lydford Gorge

National Trust property and Site of Special Scientific Interest on the edge of Dartmoor. Spectacular narrow wooded gorge where the River Lyd leaves Dartmoor granite. High Oak trees on either side meet over the waterfall called the White Lady; their trunks are overgrown with mosses, lichens and ferns. Information Centre in the car park.

□8 miles/12 km north of Tavistock off A386 via Lydford village. OS 191 or 201: 502 835.

e) Shaptor Woods

Woodland Trust. Beautiful wooded valley with several good walks, including a circular walk through mature Beech and twisted Oak; fine views from summit of Shaptor Rock. Birds include Wood Warbler and Tree Pipit.

□Keep to footpaths. Access off A382 onto unclassified road north-east of Bovey Tracey. OS 191: 819 798. Shaptor Rock, OS 191: 807 808.

f) Yarner Wood National Nature Reserve

Nature Conservancy Council. Sessile Oak woodland; nature trail through heathland and woods. Birds include Nuthatch, Woodpeckers, Pied Flycatcher, Raven, Buzzard, Wood Warbler, Blackcap and Whitethroat; typical woodland butterflies.

□Warden at Yarrow Lodge within reserve. (Tel: Bovey Tracey 832330). 15 miles/24 km south-west of Exeter. Access off A38 onto B3344 at Bovey Tracey. OS 191: 775 785.

13 Dawlish Warren

Local nature reserve with public bird-watching hide. Good dune flowers and seaside heath. Sea wall at east end of the Warren is an excellent site for watching estuary birds. In summer, look for Oyster-catcher, Turnstone, Redshank, Knot, Grey Plover, Ringed Plover, Sanderling, Dunlin, Bar-tailed Godwit, and Terns; in winter, Red-breasted Merganser, Wigeon, and Brent Geese. Wheatear, Linnet, and Stonechat can be seen in the dunes. Salt-marsh behind the Warren has Eel-Grass, Glasswort and Cord-grass, other plants in the area include Sea Storksbill, Tree Lupin, Sand Sedge, Sea Spurge, Gorse, and Sycamore thickets.

□South end of the Exe estuary, 9 miles/14 km south-east of Exeter. Access off A379. OS 192: 980 790.

14 Dunkeswell

An example of east Devon countryside well away from the more popular areas. Traditional farmland with thick hedges, scrubby slopes and damp valley bottoms.

□5 miles/8 km north of Honiton. Access along unclassified roads from A373 or A30 at Honiton. OS 192: or 193: 142 077.

15 Erme Estuary

Small estuary. Away from the popular beaches at the mouth of the river are some waders and Shelduck; Kingfisher and Greenshank in autumn.

□Midway between Plymouth and Kingsbridge. Access off A379 onto B3392 for Kingston, then along unclassified road to Wonwell Beach. Walk upstream from here to reach areas of interest. OS 202: 616 472.

16 Exe Estuary

Site of Special Scientific Interest, part bird sanctuary. Large area of mud and sand at low tide. View from Powderham, Dawlish Warren and Starcross. The walk along the sea wall from Powderham to Turf Lock is good for observing waders from August to April. Look for Goldeneye, Eider Duck, Grey Plover, Ruff, Spotted Redshank, Avocet, Slavonian and Black-necked Grebes in winter; Little Stint, Curlew Sandpiper in autumn. See also Dawlish Warren.

□Exeter to Exmouth. Access to Powderham off A379 from Exminster, then east onto unclassified road. Continue along A379 for Starcross. Powderham OS 192:

968 845; Starcross OS 192: 973 816.

Exeter Forest
See Great Haldon.

17 Exeter Royal Albert Memorial Museum and Art Gallery
Largest museum in Devon, with special Devon wildlife gallery. Local natural history information.
☐Queen Street, Exeter (Tel: Exeter 56724). Open daily, all year.

18 Farway Country Park
Extensive grounds with woodland and moorland nature trails; farm animals. Look out for Badger setts.
☐(Tel: Farway 224). Open Good Friday–September; daily except Sunday. 5 miles/8 km south of Honiton. Access off A375 onto B3174 eastwards for 2 miles/3 km; then turn left onto unclassified road. OS 192 or 193: 187 942.

19 Great Haldon (Exeter Forest)
Forestry Commission. Coniferous plantations and gravelly heath; extends southwards into Little Haldon. In some winters, plantations have visiting Redpoll, Siskin, and Crossbill. Fallow Deer; Badger. Good heath vegetation, also Early Purple and other orchids, Purging Flax, Wild Columbine, and Wild Basil. Variety of woodland flowers in deciduous woodland where Wild Service tree can be seen. Birds include Woodlark, Nightjar and Buzzard. Picnic place with views across Exe estuary; walks and nature trail. Exeter Forest booklet available from Walks Car Park and Forestry Commission Centre.
☐5 miles/8 km south of Exeter. Plateau top at 800 ft/244 m straddles A38 and A380. OS 192 or 193: 890 830.

20 Hemyock, Ashculm Turbary
Devon Trust for Nature Conservation. Site of Special Scientific Interest. Good east Devon common with typical heathland flowers and encroaching scrub.
☐5 miles/8 km south of Wellington. Access off M5 at Junction 26, then onto B3391 via Uffculme. OS 181 or 193: 120 115.

21 Ilfracombe Museum
Good collection of local flora, birds, insects, seaweed, shells, and minerals.
☐Runnymead Gardens, Ilfracombe (Tel: Ilfracombe 63541). Open daily in summer; mornings only in winter.

22 Kingsbridge Estuary
Superb salty marine inlet. Large flocks of waders and ducks in central area in winter. Good views at low tide from Bowcombe Creek Road. Look out for Wigeon in winter; Curlew, Redshank, Oystercatcher, Greenshank, Dunlin, Sandpiper, Godwits, Shelduck breed in the area. Kingfisher breeds near heads of creeks. Rich marine fauna; Knotted Wrack in lower reaches of sheltered rocky shores. Grey Mullet, Bass and Dab caught from Bowcombe Bridge.
☐20 miles/32 km east of Plymouth to Salcombe. Access off A379, south from Kingsbridge. Bowcombe Creek is branch of the estuary crossed by A379 east of Kingsbridge at OS 202: 745 433.

23 Lundy Island
Large island owned by the National Trust. Marine nature reserve. Many sea birds nest on the high granite cliffs, including Kittiwake, Fulmar and Manx Shearwater; Seals may be seen out at sea and on rocks.
☐Visitors to the Bird Observatory must be members of the Lundy Field Society. (Lundy Agent, tel: Barnstaple 73333). 11 miles/17.5 km off the north coast of Devon. Access by boat from Ilfracombe. OS sheet 180.

24 Marine Biological Association
Excellent aquarium of temperate marine life comprising fish and invertebrates; all caught locally.
☐Citadel Hill, Plymouth (Tel: Plymouth 21761). Open daily except Sunday.

25 Morwellham Open Air Museum
Industrial archaeology museum; also riverside and woodland trails, valley floor farmland, reed beds.
☐(Tel: Gunnislake 832766). 5 miles/8 km south-west of Tavistock, signposted from A390. Also access from Plymouth by boat. OS 201: 447 691.

26 Muttersmoor
Typical East Devon heathland, near coast. Stonechat. Whitethroat, Linnet; Dartford Warbler can be seen in some years. Roe Deer.
□1 mile/2 km north-west of Sidmouth. Access off Otterton road out of Sidmouth. OS 192: 105 880.

27 Otter Estuary
A small estuary in low country; much silted up; mainly saltmarsh grading into brackish marsh and fen. Good saltmarsh and maritime flowers. Look out for waders; also Kingfishers in winter.
□9 miles/14 km south-east of Exeter, on the eastern edge of Budleigh Salterton. OS 192: 076 820.

28 Paignton Zoological and Botanical Gardens
Site of Special Scientific Interest. Area of limestone and clay soils with large collection of trees and other plants, including both native and rare species. Limestone gorge in woodland. Aquarium and aviaries; collection of amphibians, reptiles, and mammals. Ducks, Pheasants, Sarus Cranes, Jungle Fowl, and other animals roam freely through the grounds.
□(Tel: Paignton 557479). Open daily, all year. East edge of Paignton on A385. OS 202: 885 598.

29 Parke
National Trust parkland. Walks from the middle of the village up the east side of the River Bovey. Floodplain meadows; Alders on stream; woodland and plantations. Good selection of meadow flowers and woodland birds. Look out for Dippers on the river. Information Centre in house, the headquarters of the Dartmoor National Park Authority.
□15 miles/24 km south-west of Exeter, on the western edge of Bovey Tracey. Access off A382 onto B3344 at Bovey Tracey. OS 191: 806 787.

30 Plym Forest
Forestry Commission. Mature coniferous woodland criss-crossed by rides. Fallow Deer in large numbers; also Badgers. Nightjar, Buzzard, Yellowhammer, and woodland birds including Greater Spotted Woodpecker and Redstart. Nature trail starts at picnic place. Leaflet available from the Forestry Commission.
□5 miles/8 km north-east of Plymouth city centre. Access off A374 onto unclassified road. OS 201: 524 590.

31 Powderham Castle
Good parkland with Fallow Deer; Woodpeckers, Nuthatches and Treecreepers. Ducks and Kingfishers on River Kenn which flows through the park. Waders visible at high water spring tide from unclassified road between the park and the Exe estuary.
□(Tel: Starcross 890243). Open Sunday, 13 April–18 May; afternoons from Sunday–Thursday, 19 May–28 September. South of Exeter off A379, onto unclassified road. OS 192: 968 845.

32 Seaton
Good base from which to explore east Devon coastline. (See especially Beer and Axmouth-Lyme Regis Landslip). It is situated at the mouth of the Axe estuary, which has interesting waterfowl in winter.
□23 miles/37 km east of Exeter. Access off A3052. OS 192 or 193: 243 900.

33 Sidmouth Cliffs
Devon Trust for Nature Conservation reserve with nature trail at Salcombe Hill; also cliff path. Good cliff-top flowers and butterflies. Leaflet available from Devon Trust for Nature Conservation.
□12 miles/19 km south-east of Exeter. Access from Sidmouth. OS 191: 140 875.

34 Slapton Ley and Slapton Sands
Site of Special Scientific Interest; nature reserve at Slapton Ley. Woodland, freshwater lagoon and 2 miles/3 km of shingle beach. Good selection of shingle flowers along the roadside, especially Yellow Horned Poppy, Bird's Foot Trefoil, Viper's Bugloss, Sea Radish, Rest-harrow, Sea Kale, Sea Holly, and the odd Sea Pea. Reed, Sedge and Cetti's Warblers breed in lakeside scrub and reed-beds in summer. Other breeding birds in the area include

Woodpecker, Raven, Buzzard, Heron, and Great Crested Grebe, Starlings roost in reed beds in winter, also Swallows and Sand Martins in autumn. Typical ducks can be seen in winter, with Pintail, Scaup and Long-tailed Duck during very cold weather. Information and guided walks from South Hams Countryside Unit at Slapton village and Torcross.

□Permits for Slapton Ley available from Slapton Ley Field Centre, Slapton, Kingsbridge, Devon. 8 miles/12 km south of Dartmouth on A379. OS 202: 820 445.

35 Start Point to Prawl Point

Rocky coastline with sandy beaches; sheltered shores just east of Prawle. Good selection of cliff-top flowers and rare lichens. Also rocky shore animals. Gulls, Stonechat, Curlew, Oystercatcher, Gannet, Shearwater and auks can be seen off both Start and Prawle Points. Start Point is a good place from which to watch sea bird migrations during autumn evenings. Flowers include Spring and Autumn Squill, Sea Carrot, Carline Thistle, Rock Samphire, Sea Beet, Sea Lavender, Bloody Cranesbill; excellent area for seaweeds.

□10 miles south-east of Kingsbridge. Both Start Point and Prawle car park (National Trust) are signposted off the A379. OS 202: 830 370 to 773 350.

36 Tamar Estuary (Devon/Cornwall Border)

Most extensive mudflats in the South-West. Good wader populations, including Avocets which regularly winter here. Other birds to look for in winter are Oystercatcher, Curlew, Knot, Dunlin, and Bar-tailed Godwit; Whimbrel, Spotted Redshank and Greenshank can be seen in autumn.

□Forms boundary of the City of Plymouth in the lower reaches; extends 12 miles/19 km north of the city. OS 201: 430 600. Good birdwatching points at:

a) Cargreen

Watch for Avocets from the quay.

□Access off A388 on northern outskirts of Saltash, onto unclassified road at Carkeel; then turn north-west at Botusfleming. OS 201: 425 626.

b) Weir Quay and Hangingcliff Woods

Overlooking the River Tamar. The wood is a Devon Trust for Nature Conservation Reserve, situated on the cliffs above Weir Quay. Fine views from here of mudflats and reed beds.

□6 miles/10 km south-west of Tavistock. Access off A390 turning south onto unclassified road 2 miles/3 km out of Tavistock; follow signposts to Bere Alston, then those to Weir Quay. OS 201: 434 648.

37 Tamar Lakes

Upper and lower lakes. Site of Special Scientific Interest and Wildfowl Refuge on lower lake. Marshy area on three sides; rich flora and fauna. Birdwatching hide.

□Access to banks and hide by permit. Contact South West Water Authority, 3–5 Barnfield Road, Exeter. 5 miles/8 km north-east of Bude from A39 at Kilkhampton. On Devon/Cornwall border. OS 190: 295 110.

38 Taw-Torridge Estuary.

Estuaries of the River Taw and River Torridge where they flow into Barnstaple Bay. Extensive mud and sand flats at low tide. Good area for birdwatching, especially waders and ducks, despite some modern development on the shores.

□Between Braunton and Northam Burrows, downstream of Barnstaple and Bideford. Vantage points for birdwatching include:

a) Appledore Quay

OS 180: 460 310.

b) Braunton Burrows

See entry on page 00.

c) Northam Burrows

OS 180: 445 319.

39 Teignmouth Museum

Good display of local seashells and minerals relating to the clay industry.

□2 French Street, Teignmouth. Open in summer, Tuesday–Friday, Sunday afternoon.

40 Tiverton Canal

County Council Country Park. This part of the Grand Western Canal runs from Tiverton to Holcombe Rogus on the Devon/

Somerset border. Walks along the tow path; horsedrawn barge excursions; nature reserve at north-east end towards Holcome Rogus. Good selection of aquatic plants and coarse fish. Leaflet from the boat in the Canal Basin at Tiverton.
☐Tiverton, OS 181: 963 123; Holcombe Rogus, OS 181: 060 180.

41 Tiverton Museum
Exhibits relating to the history of the Tiverton Canal, as well as a natural history room with examples of local fauna and geology.
☐St Andrews Street, Tiverton (Tel: Tiverton 2446). Open daily except Sunday.

42 Torbay
Area with interesting geology, good selection of rocky shore plants and animals. Berry Head (described earlier) is the best place to watch birds. Other places to visit in the area include:
a) Hope's Nose
Good for geology and birds
☐OS 202: 949 637.
b) Meadfoot Beach
Good geological structures.
☐OS 202: 931 630.
c) Saltern Cove
Site of Special Scientific Interest and Local Nature Reserve. Marine plants and animals; geology.
☐OS 202: 895 585.

43 Torquay Natural History Society Museum
Local natural history display on theme of the South Devon area during the last 400 million years. Reference collection available to researchers by appointment
☐529 Babbacombe Road, Torquay (Tel: Torquay 23975). Closed on Sundays.

44 Welcombe Mouth
Part of the nature reserve which is owned by the Society for the Promotion of Nature Conservation. Good cliff-top vegetation and coastal birds. Rocky shores; spectacular coastline exposed to the Atlantic. Resident Warden at Gooseham.
☐10 miles/16 km north of Bude. Signposted from A39. OS 190: 215 180.

45 West Exmoor
Area of coast and heather moorland in north Devon, part of Exmoor National Park (see Exmoor entry under Somerset). Brendon Valley on the north side has rich Oak coppice on steep valley sides where Wood Warblers and Flycatchers can be seen. Narrow and steepsided combes off the moorland are also good for birds, including Ring Ouzel and Wheatear. Challacombe is a good base from which to make moorland walks on The Chains.
☐Information Centres in County Gate and Combe Martin. Access off A39, B3323 and B3326. Access for Challacombe off B3358. Places of special interest in Devon are listed below.
a) Heddons Mouth
National Trust. Rich, damp woodland with nature trail through Oakwood, water-meadows, moorland, and along the sea-shore. Good area for ferns, mosses and liverworts. Leaflet from Hunters Inn Hotel.
☐Midway between Lynton and Combe Martin. Access off A399 or A39 onto narrow lanes via Trentshoe or Martinhoe. OS 180: 655 497.
b) Valley of Rocks
High valley situated above Bristol Channel. Rocky tors with heathland; Wild Goats. Good area for seeing Jackdaws, Rock Doves, sea birds and occasionally Peregrine Falcons. Fine views of the sea.
☐1 mile/2 km west of Lynton Village. Access off A39. OS 180: 705 495.
c) Watersmeet
National Trust and Site of Special Scientific Interest. Rich ground flora; many liverworts and mosses; Alder and Ash in damp places. National Trust Information Point at Watersmeet Cottage.
☐2 miles/3 km east of Lynton. Access by footpath from A39 (Lynmouth–Barnstaple road). OS 180: 746 490.
d) Woody Bay
National Trust nature reserve and Site of Special Scientific Interest. Area of cliffs, moorland and woodland. An important breeding site for auks. Peregrine Falcons often seen on the coast.
☐3 miles/5 km west of Lynton. Access off B3234 at Lynton onto unclassified road along the coast. OS 180: 675 490.

Dorset

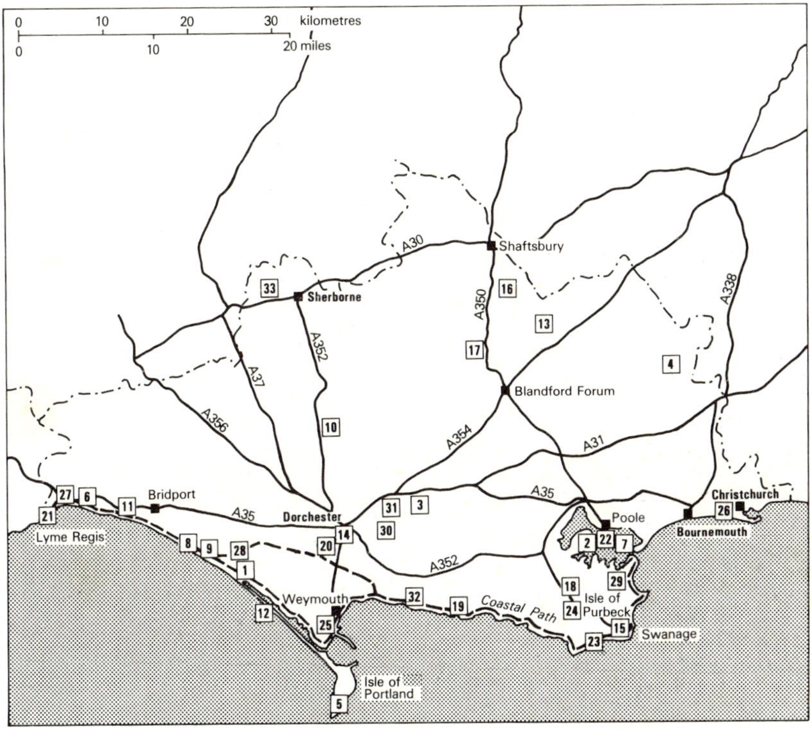

Dorset Coast Path

This footpath is part of the South-West Peninsula Coast Path, and forms the section from Lyme Regis to Poole Harbour. Starting from Lyme Regis, the first part of the path divides at West Bexington. One path then follows the coast to Abbotsbury, Langton Herring, Weymouth and Overcombe, while the other veers inland to White Horse Hill. The two join up at Osmington Mills and continue on to Poole Harbour.

☐Leaflet available from Countryside Commission. Countryside Commission guidebook is available from Her Majesty's Stationery Office. Walkers are advised to use good maps. The route is well marked on OS sheets 193, 194 and 195.

1 Abbotsbury Swannery

A swannery dating from the fourteenth century with 800 Mute Swans and many other wildfowl, including Smew and Long-tailed Duck; also Ringed Plover, Little Tern, Common Tern, and Short-eared Owl.

☐(Tel: Strangways Estate Office, Evershot 222). Open daily, May–September. Near Abbotsbury. OS 194: 575 841.

2 Arne Heath

RSPB nature reserve. Heathland, woodland and inter-tidal areas supporting typical heathland birds such as Dartford Warbler, Nightjar, Stonechat, Grasshopper Warbler, and a number of wildfowl and waders. Also reptiles, butterflies and Dragonflies. Heather, Gorse and Scots Pine grow on the reserve. Nature trail.

☐Access to Shipstal part of the reserve on public rights of way only. For permit to remaining area, apply in advance to the Warden, Syldata, Arne, Wareham. Open April–August; Wednesday, Thursday, Saturday and Sunday. Nature trail open end of May–early September. On peninsula jutting into Poole Harbour. OS 195: 970 880.

3 Athelhampton Gardens

Very fine medieval house with twelve water and architectural gardens. Rare trees and plants.

☐Puddletown (Tel: Puddletown 363). Open Easter–October, Wednesday, Thursday and Sunday afternoons; also Tuesday and Friday in August and bank holidays. Off A35, north-east of Dorchester. OS 194: 771 941.

4 Avon Forest Park

Country park of mixed heathland and Pine forest. There are good views over the Avon Valley, several woodland walks and interesting wildlife.

☐3 miles/5 km south-west of Ringwood, between A31 and A338. OS 195: 120 020.

5 Bill of Portland

The southernmost point of the Isle of Portland, a peninsula linked to the mainland by Chesil Beach. The area offers interesting geological structures and plants and is also a good place to watch birds such as Manx and Balearic Shearwaters, Chats, Flycatchers, Grebes, Warblers, Gannets, Scoters and Fulmars. Plants include Sea Lavender, Rock Samphire, Red Valerian, and Portland Spurge.

☐Off B3154 south of Weymouth. OS 194: 676 683.

6 Black Venn

National Trust and Dorset Naturalists' Trust nature reserve. Cliff, undercliff and downland. Geological features include marls, oil shales, landslips and limestone.

☐On the south-west side of Charmouth. OS 193: 356 932.

7 Brownsea Island.

National Trust. An island with woodland and heathland. The area includes a large nature reserve managed by the Dorset Naturalists' Trust, with two lakes, marshland and a beach. Red Squirrels can be seen. There is a Heronry, a Ternery, public hide, and Information Centre.

☐Access to reserve restricted to nature trail. Brownsea Island is open to the public daily from April–September. Situated in Poole Harbour, it can be reached by regular ferries from Sandbanks and Poole Quay. No dogs allowed. OS 195: 020 880.

8 Burton Cliff

National Trust. High bluff of cliff dropping down to Freshwater Bay, near the River Bridge. Pleasant cliff-top and riverside walks.

☐Near Burton Bradstock, south-east of Bridport. OS 193: 484 894.

9 Burton Mere

A drained mere overgrown with reeds; wild scrub and trees nearby. Many migrating birds can be seen in autumn – Skylark, thrushes, warblers and finches.

☐Off B3157 south-east of Burton Bradstock, which is south of Bridport. OS 194: 507 879.

10 The Cerne Giant

National Trust. An 180-ft/55-m Romano British figure cut into chalk downland, where fine examples of downland flora grow.

☐Near Cerne Abbas, 9 miles/14 km north of Dorchester on A352. Best seen from A352 lay-by north of the village. OS 194: 666 017.

11 Chardown, Stonebarrow and the Undercliffs

National Trust and Dorset Naturalists' Trust nature reserve. A wide stretch of farmland, downland and cliffs.

☐Off A35 Charmouth-Bridport road. OS 193: 395 935.

12 Chesil Beach and The Fleet

Area of shingle reef and brackish lagoons. Breeding birds are Common and Little Terns, and Ringed Plovers. Large numbers of Wigeon in winter. Flowers include Sea Holly, Sea Pea, Sea Rocket, Seablite and Sea Kale.

☐No access to Ternery in the breeding season. Chesil Beach reached via B1357 from Abbotsbury or A354 from Portland. OS 194: 565 845 to 675 735.

13 Cranborne Chase

Extensive stretches of woodland, mainly Oak trees and Beech trees, growing on chalk and clay-with-flint soils. Fallow, Roe and Sika Deer may be seen. Many woodland flowers, especially where there is Hazel coppicing.
□North-east of Blandford Forum, on B3081. OS 195: 900 130.

14 Dorset County Museum

Dorset geology, natural history, local history and archaeology exhibits.
□High Street, Dorchester (Tel: Dorchester 2735). Open Monday–Saturday, all year.

15 Durlston Country Park

The park includes Durlston Head, a good birdwatching site. Downland and limestone cliffs with colonies of gulls and Kittiwakes. Coastal and limestone flowers include Sea Campion, Yellow Centaury and orchids. Fossils can be seen. There are guided walks, an Information Centre and car parks.
□On the south-east corner of the Isle of Purbeck. South of Swanage. OS 195: 031 773.

16 Fontmell Downs

National Trust and Dorset Naturalists' Trust. Unimproved downland with fine views across the Blackmore Vale. There is an Iron Age cross dyke and good downland flora.
□Off A350 Shaftesbury-Blandford Forum, near Fontmell Magna. OS 183: 884 184.

17 Hod Hill

An ancient monument set on chalk downland where butterflies and orchids can be seen. Access is restricted to the bridle path.
□4 miles/6.5 km north of Blandford Forum. Access off A350. OS 194: 855 108.

18 Isle of Purbeck

The landscape includes chalk and limestone ridges and clay vales. Downland. Interesting flora and farmland wildlife can be seen in the area.
□South of Wareham. Access off A351. OS 195: 940 820.

19 Lulworth Cove

A famous cove of interest to geologists. Fossils can be seen and good limestone flowers grow nearby.
□Access off A352 Wareham-Weymouth road onto B3070. OS 194: 826 797.

20 Maiden Castle

Large Iron Age hill fort surrounded by sweeping downland turf with good downland flowers. Corn Buntings breed in the area.
□1½ miles/2.5 km south-west of Dorchester. Access off A354. OS 194: 666 884.

21 Philpot Museum

West Dorset fossils, geology and archaeology.
□Bridge Street, Lyme Regis (Tel: Lyme Regis 3370). Open daily, Easter–September; October–Easter, weekends, Tuesday morning and Thursday afternoon.

22 Poole Harbour

Good birdwatching area. The wide estuary of the Frome and Piddle Rivers. Saltmarsh and a wide variety of waders and Grebes, especially in winter. Vantage points for birdwatching include:
a) South Haven Point
OS 195: 036 868.
b) Rockley Sands Caravan Site
OS 195: 977 909.

Portland Bill

See Bill of Portland.

23 Purbeck Cliffs

Spectacular limestone cliffs. A good place to see breeding seabirds such as Puffin, Fulmar, Razorbill, Guillemot and Kittiwake. Black Redstarts are winter visitors.
□Access on foot from Swanage and Durlstone Head; follow path past lighthouses to St Aldhelm's Head. OS 195: 960 750 to 030 770.

24 Purbeck Marine Wildlife Reserve

Dorset Naturalists' Trust. Shale cliffs around Kimmeridge Bay; rich in fossils. Many seabirds and a good selection of marine wildlife.
□For details, contact Dorset Naturalists'

Trust, 39 Christchurch Road, Bournemouth (Tel: Bournemouth 24241). Reserve is south-west of Corfe Castle. OS 195: 900 790.

25 Radipole Lake

RSPB nature reserve. A wildfowl refuge on an area of reed beds and lagoons. There is a breeding colony of Bearded Tits. Reed Warblers and Sedge Warblers are summer visitors; winter wildfowl include Pintail, Pochard, Shoveler and, occasionally, Bittern.

□For information contact the Warden, 52 Goldcroft Avenue, Weymouth. Within built-up area of Weymouth. Access on foot from Swannery car park. OS 194: 670 800.

26 Red House Museum and Art Gallery

Local natural history and geology displays. There are roses and a herb garden in the grounds.

□Christchurch (Tel: Christchurch 482860). Open Tuesday–Sunday, all year; closed Sunday mornings.

27 The Spittles

National Trust and Dorset Naturalists' Trust nature reserve. Coastal site with cliffs.

□On the north-east side of Lyme Regis. OS 193: 350 930.

28 Studland Heath National Nature Reserve

Nature Conservancy Council. Heathland, dunes, Birch woodland and boggy ground; also a freshwater lagoon with a birdwatching hide. Sand Lizard, Adder, Smooth Snake, Grayling Butterfly and Tiger Beetle can be seen, as well as a large number of winter ducks. Sea Sandwort, Sea Rocket, Royal Fern and Heathers grow on the reserve. Nature trails; leaflets available on the site.

□4 miles/6.5 km north of Swanage. Access off A35 onto B3352. OS 195: 020 830.

29 Sub-tropical Gardens

Open gardens with unusual and rare shrubs and trees.

□Abbotsbury (Tel: Strangways Estate Office, Evershot 222). Open daily, mid-March to mid-October.

30 Thorncombe Wood

Area of heath and mixed woodland, cut across by a Roman road. There are various walks, nature trails, and information boards. Leaflets available on the site.

□3 miles/5 km east of Dorchester, south of A35, near Hardy's Cottage at Higher Bockhampton. OS 194: 720 920.

31 Wareham Forest

Forestry Commission. Extensive woodland of mixed conifers and broadleaved trees with wide stretches of heath. Badgers, Sika Deer, Grasshoppers and Dragonflies may be seen. Several waymarked walks (guide available on the site) and pleasant picnic spots, especially north of Wareham and around Affpuddle and Puddletown. These include:

a) Puddletown Picnic Place

A large site on the edge of mixed woods, mainly of Larch and Beech trees, with a forest trail.

□Near Beacon Corner, off A35 south-west of Puddletown. OS 194: 745 936.

b) Coldharbour Picnic Place

Pine woodland on Dorset heathland with a forest trail going past an arboretum.

□1 mile/1.6 km north-west of Wareham level crossing on Bere Regis road. OS 195: 905 894.

32 Whitenothe Cliff

National Trust and Dorset Naturalists' Trust. Nature reserve on Chalk and Greensand cliff, with a path along the edge of Ringstead Bay. Good flowers and fossils can be seen here.

□4 miles/6.5 km east off Weymouth, off A353. OS 194: 760 810.

33 Worldwide Butterflies.

A butterfly farm housed in Compton House, also the site of Lullingstone Silk Farm. There are caterpillars and pupae for sale, and many live butterflies, both British and foreign on show.

□Compton House, near Sherborne (Tel: Yeovil 4608). Open daily, April–October. OS 183: 594 167.

Somerset

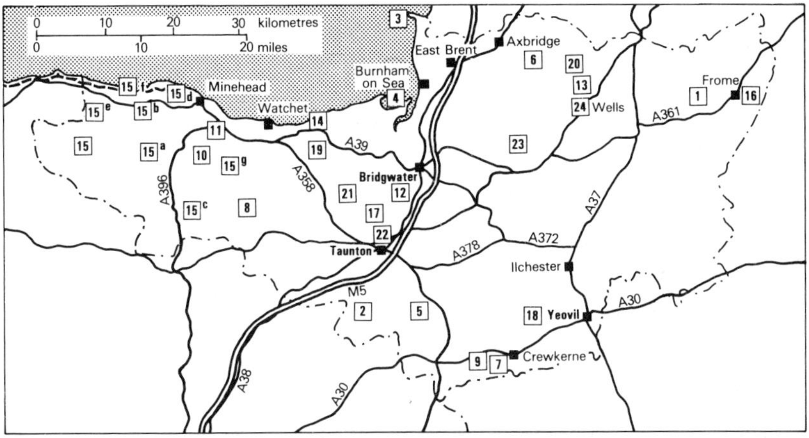

Somerset and North Devon Coast Path
This long distance path from Minehead in Somerset to Marsland Mouth on the Devon/Cornwall border is part of the South-West Peninsula Coast Path. Much of the route follows the coast, giving fine views of the sea. From Minehead to Combe Martin it passes through the beautiful landscape of Exmoor National Park; from there it continues through the North Devon Area of Outstanding Natural Beauty. Areas of particular interest along the path in Somerset are described below.
□Leaflet about the path from the Countryside Commission. Guidebooks on the Exmoor route from National Park Information Centres at Minehead, Lynmouth and Combe Martin or Exmoor National Park Office, Exmoor House, Dulverton, Somerset. Walkers should take good maps as the waymarking along some parts of the path is incomplete. The route is well marked on OS 180, 181 and 190.

1 Ammerdown Nature Trail
Walk through mixed native woodland and conifer plantation, in Ammerdown Park. Superb views of eastern Mendips; good selection of birds, butterflies and plants. Trail leaflet available on site.
□Trail starts and ends in car park at Terry Hill crossroads on A362, 2½ miles/4 km south-east of Radstock. OS 183: 715 535.

2 Black Down Hills
Range of hills along the Devon/Somerset border. Heathland, bog and acid woodland on upper plateau; calcareous grassland and woodland on north-facing scarp slope. Large tract of wood includes ancient coppice woods of Oak and Ash with Wild Service tree and Small-leaved Lime; rich woodland ground flora.
□South of Taunton on B3170, then turn east near Staple Hill. OS 193: 230 163.

3 Brean Down
National Trust. Headland forming the south arm of Weston Bay. The Down is a resting place for migrating birds crossing the Bristol Channel; rare White Rockrose can be seen in profusion on the sea cliffs. Descriptive booklet available from the Somerset Trust for Nature Conservation.
□2 miles/3 km south of Weston-super-Mare. Access off A38 at East Brent onto B3140 to Berrow; then north along coast road through Brean. OS 182: 297 587.

4 Bridgwater Bay National Nature Reserve
Nature Conservancy Council. Coastal shingle, saltmarsh and mudflats from Hinkley Point to Stert Island. Excellent area for watching birds, especially wintering waders and wildfowl, breeding Oystercatchers, and Ringed Plover. One of the largest

Shelduck moulting sites in Britain. Several observation hides.

□Permits necessary for some hides. Contact Nature Conservancy Council Regional Office, Roughmoor, Bishop's Hull, Taunton, Somerset. Off A39, 3 miles/ 4.5 km west of Bridgwater at Cannington; then by unclassified road to Steart. OS 182: 275 458.

5 Castle Neroche Nature Trail

Forestry Commission. Trail in the Neroche Forest, an area of varied deciduous and coniferous woodland with open patches of heath.

□Access off B3170, 7 miles/11 km south of Taunton or north off A303 near Buckland St Mary. OS 193: 274 157.

6 Cheddar Gorge

Gorge in Mendip limestone. Extensive system of underground stream and caves. Cliffs and screes support rare plants such as Cheddar Pink, Limestone Polypody, Brittle Bladder Fern, and Lesser Meadow-rue.

□Access off A371 from Axbridge to Wells, onto B3135 in Cheddar which runs up through the gorge. OS 182: 470 540. The following places are also of interest:

a) Black Rock Nature Trail

Somerset Trust for Nature Conservation. Nature trail around the Black Rock Reserve, an area of limestone downland, scree, scrub and woodland. Interesting selection of birds and insects; plants include Autumn Gentian, Slender Bedstraw and Common Rockrose. Trail leaflet available on the site.

□At upper end of Cheddar Gorge. Entrance and car park at Black Rock Gate on B3135. OS 182: 483 546.

b) Cheddar Caves Museum and Exhibition

Diaramas of lead smelting; exhibitions of local finds, how cave man lived. Also walks through some of the caves.

□Cheddar village (Tel: Cheddar 742343). Open daily, Easter–October.

c) Long Wood Nature Trail

Somerset Trust for Nature Conservation. Walk around ancient Ash, Hazel, Maple woodland, managed as coppice with standards. Very good for spring flowers, also Herb Paris and Autumn Crocus. Birds include Treecreeper, Tree Pipit, Nuthatch, Woodpeckers, Grasshopper Warbler, Redstart, and Sparrowhawk. Trail leaflet available at the site.

□At the head of the Cheddar Gorge. Access from car park at Black Rock Gate. OS 182: 483 585:.

d) Velvet Bottom

Somerset Trust for Nature Conservation. Reserve and nature trail. Remains of Roman lead smelting works and nineteenth-century slag tips with an unusual grassland community, determined by the very high lead content in the soil. Slag heaps support plants typical of seashore and alpine conditions; valley sides are of limestone grassland and scrub. Nature trail leaflet available on the site.

□Entrance at Black Rock Gate or from the Charterhouse-Priddy road, OS 182: 503 555.

7 Clapton Court

Formal woodland gardens with rare shrubs and trees.

□(Tel: Crewkerne 73220). Open 23 March–31 October, Sunday–Friday, afternoons only. 3 miles/4.5 km south of Crewkerne on B3165. OS 193: 412 068.

8 Clatworthy Reservoir

Wessex Water Authority. The reservoir is fringed by grassland, marshland and woodland, parts of which are on the route of the nature trail. Birds include Redstart, Pied Flycatcher, Buzzard and Heron; also breeding and wintering wildfowl. Viewing area; picnic site.

□Trail starts at the dam. 5 miles/8 km north-west of Wiveliscombe off A361 onto minor road via Huish Champflower. South of Watchet. OS 181: 043 310.

9 Cricket St Thomas Wildlife Park

Large area of parkland with interesting collection of animals. Woodland walk; geese and wildfowl on the lakes.

□Open daily, all year. 3 miles/4.5 km east of Chard on A30. OS 193: 375 085.

10 Croydon Hill

Forestry Commission. Forest and open heathland. Good walks; fine views over

Exmoor and the Bristol Channel from the summit of Black Hill. Redpolls are abundant in mature conifers; Chats and Pipits can be seen in the clearings. Look for Nightjars on summer evenings.
□4 miles/6.5 km south of Minehead. Access from A396. OS 181: 987 395.

11 Dunster Castle
National Trust. Fourteenth-century castle; gardens and deer park. Fine views of the sea. Sub-tropical plants grow along the terraced woodland walks.
□(Tel: Dunster 314). Open April–September, daily except Friday and Saturday. 3 miles/4.5 km south-east of Minehead off A39. OS 181: 995 435.

12 Durleigh Reservoir
Wessex Water Authority. Mudflats at the head of the reservoir are exposed in summer, providing good feeding areas for waders: Wood and Green Sandpipers, Spotted Redshank, Ruff, Terns and Little Gull. Breeding birds include Great Crested Grebe, Reed Warbler, Gadwall.
□Key to bird hide from fishing lodge at the south end of the dam. Follow signposts to Durleigh from A39 in Bridgwater. There are good views of the reservoir from the Durleigh–Enmore road. OS 182: 270 362.

13 East Quantoxhead
Cliffs and rocky shore with coastal path to limestone downland. Typical coastal flowers; interesting limestone and clay structures.
□3½ miles/5.5 km east of Watchet. Access off A39 onto unclassified road to East Quantoxhead village, where there is a car park. Walk north on footpath to coast. OS 181: 137 435.

14 Ebbor Gorge
National Nature Reserve
National Trust; managed by the Nature Conservancy Council. 142 acres/57 ha of well-wooded limestone gorge. Rich flora typical of lime soils; nature trail. Leaflet available from the car park.
□2 miles/3 km north-west of Wells. Access off A371 onto unclassified road in Wells or at Haybridge. OS 182: 530 490.

15 Exmoor National Park
(Somerset and Devon)
Area of 265 square miles/686 square km, two-thirds of which are in Somerset. Beautiful cliffed and wooded coast; inland, there is heather and grass moorland with occasional strips of woodland occupying the steep-sided river valleys of the Exe, Barle, Quarme, Haddeo, Avill, and Aller.
□Information Centres in Dulverton, Minehead, County Gate and Combe Martin. OS sheets 180 and 181. Places of special interest in Somerset are listed below. (See also West Exmoor under Devon.)

a) Dunkery Hill
National Trust. Area of heather moorland with fine views from Dunkery Beacon, at 1700 ft/520 m, the highest point on Exmoor. Birds include Red Grouse, Buzzard and Curlew; Hobby can occasionally be seen hunting Meadow Pipit and Skylark. Cloutsham Nature Trail, on the north side of the hill, is a circular walk through Oakwoods and over moorland. Trail leaflet from Exmoor National Park Information Centres or Somerset Trust for Nature Conservation.
□Cloutsham Nature Trail starts at the car park at Webber's Point. OS 181: 903 440. 7 miles/11.5 km south-west of Minehead. Access to Beacon off A396 at Wheddon Cross onto B3224, then turn north onto Luccombe and Stoke Pero road. OS 181: 892 415.

b) Horner Woods
National Trust. Ancient woods in the network of valleys around Horner Water. Mainly Oak forest with Ash, Alder, Elm, and Hazel stands; also old Oak coppices. Woodland birds include Redstart, Wood Warbler, Pied Flycatcher, Dipper, and Ring Ouzel. Rich selection of flora, especially lichens. Several good walks.
□Off A39, 1 mile/1.6 km east of Porlock, onto unclassified road signposted Horner and Luccombe. Car park in orchard at OS 181: 897 455.

c) Hurscombe Nature Trail,
Wimbleball Lake
The lake is a new reservoir, managed by the South West Water Authority; flooded in 1980, it occupies the upper valley of the

River Haddeo. Hurscombe Reserve is leased to the Somerset Trust for Nature Conservation. It is managed to create a variety of woodland, scrub and grassland habitats for birds, plants and insects. Many trees and shrubs have been planted and grazing arranged to maintain the marsh pastures. Breeding waterfowl include Shelduck, Mallard, Coot; visiting wildfowl include White-fronted Goose, Teal, Pochard, Wigeon, Scaup, Goosander. Wintering waders are also of interest. Leaflet available at the start.

□Trail starts at Bessom Bridge car park, on unclassified road 1½ miles/2.5 km east of Brompton Regis. Footpaths to most of reservoir, many through deciduous woodland. OS 181: 975 317.

d) North Hill, Minehead

Area stretching from Minehead west to Hurlestone Point and Bossington village. Cliff path is good for watching birds – mostly gulls and Oystercatchers, occasionally Peregrine Falcons. Look for Whitethroat, Stonechat and Wood Warbler in autumn. Interesting coastal flora below; heathland above on the hill. Nature trail; leaflet available from the National Park Information Centres or the Somerset Trust for Nature Conservation.

□North Hill Nature Trail starts at the car park by Minehead Harbour. OS 181: 970 473.

e) Oare Valley

Valley of Chalk Water and Weir Water. Wooded downstream; open moorland in the headwaters. Dipper, Ring Ouzel on stream sides; Wheatear, Stonechat and Whinchat on the moor.

□Off A39 between Porlock and Lynton. OS 181: 815 464.

f) Porlock Bay

Long shingle beach with rich variety of shingle plants on the backslope. Porlock Marsh lies behind the beach; Redshank, Lapwing, Ringed Plover and Curlew on the ponds and brackish meadows.

□Access of Porlock Weir road from Porlock (B3225). Walk to beach from the car park. OS 181: 867 477.

g) Roadwater Valley

Beautiful wooded valley upstream of Roadwater to Luxborough. Streamside birds include Dipper, Grey Wagtail, Kingfisher, Marsh Tit; Buzzard and Sparrowhawk in adjoining woodland. Rich meadow flora in some areas, with Meadowsweet and Hemlock Water Dropwort.

□Off A39 at Washford, 5 miles/8 km south-east of Minehead, onto unclassified road to Roadwater. OS 181: 028 381.

16 Frome and East Mendip Museum

A fine collection of local minerals, fossils and rock types, representing the varied geological past of the area. Also displays of archaeology and local history.

□Wine Street, Frome (Tel: Frome 2264). Open March–November, Wednesday, Friday and Saturday; December–February, Wednesday and Saturday only.

17 Fyne Court

Headquarters of Somerset Trust for Nature Conservation, in buildings and grounds owned by the National Trust. Interpretation Centre with exhibits of Quantock wildlife, geology and local land-use pressures. Woodland walks; nature trails.

□Broomfield. Grounds and buildings open every afternoon. Signposted from direction of Kingston St Mary, Bridgwater and North Petherton.

18 Hamdon Hill Country Park

Extensive quarries on the hilltop are the source of Ham stone from which many of the local houses are built. Interesting limestone plants on the old quarry spoil tips and surrounding pasture.

□7 miles/11 km east of Ilminster. Access off A3088 onto unclassified road at Stoke sub Hamdon. OS 193: 478 172.

19 Hodder's and Holford Combes

Deep wooded valleys at the north-east end of the Quantock Hills. Mature Sessile Oak woodland and old Oak coppice. Typical woodland birds; plants of acid woodland. Good area for Red Deer. Walks along bridlepaths through woods and surrounding heather moorland on Longstone Hill, Hare Knap and Dowsborough.

□10 miles/16 km west of Bridgwater, off A39. Access from car park at Holford Bowling Green. OS 181: 155 410.

20 Mendip Hills
Long range of hills from Weston-super-Mare to Shepton Mallet, mainly of Carboniferous Limestone. The western part is most dramatic, with steep, often wooded or scrub-covered slopes and flat or rounded hill tops. The eastern Mendip is extensively quarried and dissected by steep river valleys of the Mells, Whatley Brook, Nunney Brook and Frome. There are good examples of ancient woods, limestone grasslands, cliffs, screes, and disused mines, all with interesting wildlife. See also Cheddar Gorge, Ebbor Gorge Nature Trail, Frome and East Mendip Museums, Wells Museum.
□OS sheets 182 and 183.

21 Quantock Hills
An Area of Outstanding Natural Beauty, parts of which are administered by the National Trust, Forestry Commission and local Council. Ridge of Old Red Sandstone running from west of Bridgwater to just north of Taunton. Open heathland with wooded valleys in the northern half; mainly agricultural land at the southern end.
□Somerset County Council Information Centre at Nether Stowey Library, Nether Stowey. Open Monday, Wednesday and Friday. Access to the hills from car park above West Quantoxhead, off A39. OS 181: 117 411. The following places in the area are of interest to visitors:

a) Aisholt Ring Walk
Somerset Trust for Nature Conservation. Circular walk around Aisholt Common. Leaflet available from the Somerset Trust for Nature Conservation at Fyne Court.
□Walk begins from the car park at Birches Corner. Access off A358 via West Bagborough OS 181: 182 338.

b) Quantock Forest Walk
Forestry Commission trail. Booklet available on site. The Somerset Trust also has a walk around the southern half of Great Wood. Leaflet available from the Somerset Trust for Nature Conservation at Fyne Court.
□Access to Forestry Commission trail off A39 at Nether Stowey OS 181: 176 375. The Somerset Trust walk starts and ends at Triscombe Stone car park. Access off A358 via Crowcombe. OS 181: 165 360.

22 Somerset County Museum
Collection of birds and mammals; aquarium. Displays of local natural history interests; very important local collection of rocks and minerals. Comprehensive local history and natural history library. Headquarters of the Somerset Archaeological and Natural History Society.
□Taunton Castle, Taunton (Tel: Taunton 73415 extn 374). Open weekdays; closed Mondays in winter.

23 Somerset Levels
Approximately 165 square miles/427 square km of low-lying flat land in central Somerset (see page 32). Winter flooding in the area is often prolonged, creating excellent conditions for Bewick's Swans, White-fronted Geese, and other wintering waders and wildfowl. High water levels in spring and early summer enable Snipe, Redshank, Yellow Wagtail, Lapwing, and Curlew to breed in large numbers. Rich meadow flora in some areas. The best areas to visit are King's Sedgemoor, Chiltern Moors, Tealham/Tadham Moor, Southlake Moor, Wet Moor, and West Sedgemoor. Keep to the public rights of way as all of this land is farmland.
□OS sheets 182, 183, 193.
a) Somerset Peat Moors
Former raised bog sites on the Somerset Levels. The *Sphagnum* peat deposits are colonized by acid heath plants: Ling, Bell Heather, Cross-leaved Heath, Common Sundew, Bog Asphodel, Purple Moor-grass, and Sweet Gale.
□Areas of peat bog for viewing at Sharpham, Meare, and Westhay. OS 182: 460 390, 450 400, 450 440.

24 Wells Museum
Local wildlife; comprehensive geology collection; display about Mendip mining history.
□Cathedral Green, Wells (Tel: Wells 73477). Open daily in summer, Monday–Saturday afternoons in winter.

Conservation

Britain still offers a variety of habitats rich in wildlife, and areas of wild and beautiful countryside; but these areas are threatened as more land is taken up by industry, housing and agriculture.

When hedgerows are removed and woodlands are cleared, wetlands drained, heaths replaced by forestry plantations, and trees felled indiscriminately, vital habitats are destroyed. The aim of wildlife conservation is to preserve existing habitats and manage them so as to ensure that the species dependent upon these habitats survive.

In Britain the official organization for the conservation of wildlife is the Nature Conservancy Council. They seek to inform farmers, planners and industrialists about environmental problems and to gain their co-operation in caring for the environment. The Council also protects important habitats by setting aside certain areas as nature reserves.

The ultimate responsibility for the survival of our wildlife lies with everyone, if the variety of countryside and wildlife is to remain and be enjoyed by future generations. The Countryside Commission has drawn up guidelines for visitors to the countryside. The main points are listed below.

The Country Code

Guard against all risk of fire.
Fasten all gates.
Keep dogs under proper control.
Keep to the paths across farm land.
Avoid damaging fences, hedges, walls.
Leave no litter.
Safeguard water supplies.
Protect wildlife, wild plants and trees.
Go carefully on country roads.
Respect the life of the countryside.

● *The Conservation of Wild Creatures and Wild Plants Act* makes it illegal to pick certain plants which are so rare as to be endangered, and to uproot *any wild plant* without the landowner's permission.

● *The Bird Protection Act* makes it illegal to take the eggs or disturb any wild bird at its nest.

Nature Conservation in the West Country

All parts of the West Country are rich in wildlife. The impression of luxuriance and variety lulls the observer into a mood of "all's well" with this world. However, farmers are under pressure to improve their methods of farming. The change from traditional dairying to arable farming is financially encouraged by the government. So as arable acres increase, pastures are ploughed up and hedges, walls and trees are removed. Commercial digging of limestone, peat, china clay and roadstone also results in the removal of habitats.

Tourism, the second largest industry in the region, creates two further pressures. It causes semi-urban development – roads, caravan and camping sites, the spread of coastal resorts, and the pylons and reservoirs necessary to service them. The second pressure is the innocent disturbance and damage which visitors to the countryside cause. On popular approaches to beaches and scenic viewpoints you can see the physical damage to vegetation.

Local authorities try to manage such places to reduce the impact but everyone – especially those who buy this book – should take greater care than they have done so far, to minimise the disturbance. Take care where you park or picnic, do not go searching for "rare" species, try to remember that nature reserves exist for the wildlife, not for visitors. "Take only photographs, leave only footprints" is still a good code.

In Britain the Sand Crocus is now restricted to and protected in one Devon nature reserve.

Useful Addresses

Countryside Commission, John Dower House, Crescent Place, Cheltenham, Glos. (South-West Regional Office), Bridge House, Sion Place, Clifton Down, Bristol, Avon
Field Studies Council (Courses, mainly residential, for amateur naturalists), Information Office, Preston Montford, Montford Bridge, Shrewsbury, Salop
□The Leonard Wills Field Centre, Nettlecombe Court, Williton, Taunton, Somerset
□Slapton Ley Field Centre, Slapton, Kingsbridge, Devon
Forestry Commission, S. W. Conservancy, Flowers Hill, Brislington, Bristol, Avon
National Trust (Devon and Cornwall Information Office), Saltram, Plympton, Plymouth, Devon. (Somerset and Dorset Information Office), Stourhead, Stourton, Warminster, Wilts.
Nature Conservancy Council (South-West Region), Roughmoor, Bishop's Hull, Taunton, Somerset
RSPB (Royal Society for the Protection of Birds), The Lodge, Sandy, Beds. (South-West England Office), 10 Richmond Road, Exeter, Devon
Society for the Promotion of Nature Conservation, The Green, Nettleham, Lincoln, Lincs.
Southern Tourist Board (East Dorset), Old Town Hall, Leigh Road, Eastleigh, Hants.
West Country Tourist Board, (Cornwall, Devon, Somerset, West Dorset), Trinity Court, 37 Southernhay East, Exeter, Devon
Woodland Trust, Butterbrook, Harford, Ivybridge, Devon

Cornwall Birdwatching and Preservation Society, Lewidden, Penrose, St Ervan, Wadebridge, Cornwall
Cornwall Naturalists' Trust, Trendrine, Zennor, St Ives, Cornwall
Devon Birdwatching and Preservation Society, Uplands, Looseleigh Lane, Crownhill, Plymouth, Devon
Devon Trust for Nature Conservation, 75 Queen Street, Exeter, Devon
Dorset Birdwatching Club, Manor House, Bagber, Sturminster Newton, Dorset
Dorset Naturalists' Trust, 39 Christchurch Road, Bournemouth, Dorset
Somerset Ornithological Society, Barnfield, Tower Hill Road, Crewkerne, Somerset
Somerset Trust for Nature Conservation, Fyne Court, Broomfield, Bridgwater, Somerset

Further Reading

Beside the Sea. Tony & Hilary Soper (BBC Publications: 1979)
Dartmoor. L. A. Harvey & D. St Leger (Collins: 1974)
Geology Explained: Dartmoor and the Tamar Valley. J. W. Perkins (David & Charles: 1977)
"Historic Houses, Castles and Gardens in Great Britain and Ireland" (ABC Publications: Magazine published annually)
The Naturalist in Central Southern England. Derrick Knowlton (David & Charles: 1973)
The Naturalist in Devon and Cornwall. Roger Burrows (David & Charles: 1971)
Nature in the West Country. S. A. Manning (World's Work: 1979)
The Penguin Dictionary of British Natural History. Richard & Maisie Fitter (Penguin Books: 1967)
Wildlife in Cornwall and the Isles of Scilly. Rennie Bere (D. Bradford Barton: 1973)
Wildlife of the Land's End Peninsula. (Cornwall County Council)
The Birds of Britain and Europe. Heinzel, Fitter & Parslow (Collins: 1972)
Where to Watch Birds. John Gooders (Deutsch: 1974)
British Butterflies. Robert Godden (David & Charles: 1978)
Flowers of the Coast. Ian Hepburn (Collins New Naturalist series: 1972)
Flowers of the Cornish Coast. J. A. Paton (Tor Mark Press)
The Wild Flowers of Britain and Northern Europe. Fitter, Fitter & Blamey (Collins: 1978)

Index

Page numbers in bold refer to illustrations. Place names appearing in "Places to Visit" are generally listed under the appropriate category (eg. nature reserves, zoos, country parks).

Aaron's Rod, 58
Adder, 18, **21**, 31, 102, 104, 116
Agrimony, Fragrant, 103
  Hemp, **22**, **68**
Alder, Common, **92**, **96**
Alexander, 10
Ammonite, **6**
Anemone, Sea, 13, 102
  Beadlet, **84**
  Dahlia, **84**
  Daisy, **84**
  Hermit Crab, **84**
  Snakelocks, **84**
Anemone, Wood, **72**
aquarium, 110
Ash, Common, **92**, **96**
Ashburton, 28
Ashwood, 25
Asparagus, Wild, 102
Aspen, **93**, **96**
Asphodel, Bog, **21**, 32, 121
Aster, Sea, 17, **17**, **62**, 106
aviary, 110
Avocet, **16**, 108, 36

Badger, 3, 20, 25, 30, 38, 100, 109, 116
  sett, **25**, 109
Barnacle, 13, **13**
  Acorn, **87**
  Star, **87**
Basil, Wild, 109
Bass, 109
Bartsia, Yellow, 102
Bat, 28
  Daubenton's, 99
  Greater Horsehoe, 28, **29**
  Natterer's, 99
Bedstraw, Heath, 18, 30
  Marsh, 101
  Slender, 118
Beech, Common, 20, 24, **94**, **96**
Beechwood, 24
Beet, Sea, 101, 111
Beetle, Tiger, **31**, 116
Bellflower, Clustered, 29, **29**
Berry Head, 10, 28, 106
Betony, 99
Bilberry, 20, **21**, 24, 30, **67**
Bindweed, Greater, **64**
  Sea, **65**, 103
Birch, 30
  Silver, 20, **93**, **96**
Bistort, 26, **64**
Bittern, 116
Bittersweet, 101
Blackbird, **48**
Blackcap, **46**, 107, 108
Blackthorn, 10
Bladderwort, Greater, **32**
Blenny, 13, **14**, 103
Blue Anchor Bay, 5
Bluebell, 24, **63**
Bobolink, 102
Bodmin Moor, 4, 26, 98
bog, 18, 32
  blanket, 18
  peat, 32
  valley, 18
Bog-rush, Black, 102
Bolt Tail, 4
Boscastle, **6**
Bovey Basin, 30
Bracken, 18
Braunton Burrows, 15, **15**
Bramble, 10, **78**
Brittle Star, 17
  Common, **87**
  Small, **87**
Brooklime, **63**
Broom, **59**
  Butcher's, 102, 103
  Prostrate, 99
Broomrape, 10
Bryony, White, **73**
Buckfastleigh, 28
Buckthorn, Sea, 101
Bugle, **63**
Bugloss, Viper's, 15, **15**, **62**, 101, 110
Bullfinch, 51
Bulrush, 26
Bunting, Cirl, 23
  Corn, 29, **52**, 115
  Reed, **52**
Burnet, Salad, 29, 106
Butterbur, 103
Buttercup, Bulbous, **57**
  Creeping, **57**
Butterfly, Admiral, Red, **80**, 103
  Admiral, White, 24, 106
  Blue, Common, **81**, 99, 103, 104, 107
  Blue, Chalkhill, **29**
  Brimstone, **82**
  Brown, Wall, **79**
  Clouded Yellow, 10, 99, 104
  Copper, Small, **81**, 103
  Fritillary, 107
  Fritillary, Heath, **25**
  Fritillary, Silver-washed, 24, 102
  Grayling, 31, **79**, 99, 116
  Hairstreak, Green, 103
  Heath, Small, **79**
  Orange Tip, **81**
  Painted Lady, 10, **80**, 99, 104, 107
  Peacock, **80**, 107
  Skipper, Lulworth, 29
  Speckled Wood, 24
  Tortoiseshell, Small, **80**, 107
  White, Green-veined, **82**
  White, Large, **81**
  White, Small, **82**
Butterwort, 98
Buzzard, 18, **19**, **37**, 101, 102, 103, 106, 107, 108, 109, 111, 119

Cabbage, Wild, 10
Campion, Bladder, **76**
  Red, **22**, **68**
  Sea, 10, 28, **76**, 103, 115
  White, **76**
Canal, Tiverton (Grand Western), 9, **26**, 27, 111
canals, 9, 27
Carn Brea, 4
Carnmenellis, 4
Carrot, Sea, 102, 106, 111
  Wild, **74**
Celandine, Lesser, **57**
Centaury, Common, **66**
  Yellow, 115
Chat, 106, 114, 119, *see also* under individual species
Chaffinch, **50**
chalk, 4, **4**, 5, 28–29
Cheddar Gorge, 28, **29**, 118
Chervil, Rough, 104
Chesil Beach, 7, 15, 114
Chestnut, Horse, **95–96**
  Sweet, **95–96**
Chickweed, **76**
Chiffchaff, **47**, 104
Cinquefoil, Creeping, **60**
  Marsh, 100
clay, 4, **4**, **5**
  china, 4, **7**
Clematis, 106
cliffs, 4, 5, **5**, **8–9**
  birds of, 10
  plants of, 10, **11**
climate, 7
  arctic, 5
clitter, 20
Clover, Burrowing, 103
  Large Lizard, 102
  White, **75**
Club-rush, 107
coast, 4–5, 10–15
Coast Path (South-West Peninsula), Cornwall, 98, **98**
  Dorset, 113, **113**
  Somerset and North Devon, 117, **117**
  South Devon, 105, **105**
Cockle, 17
  Edible, **86**
Columbine, Wild, 109
Coot, **37**
Cord-grass, 17, 108
Cormorant, 10, **12**, 17, **34**, 100, 104, 106
Cotton Grass, 18
country parks,
  Avon Forest Park, 114
  Berry Head, 106
  Durlstone Country Park, 115
  Farway Country Park, 109
  Hamdon Hill Country Park, 120
  Tiverton Canal, 111
Cowrie, 13
Cowslip, **57**, 101
Cow-wheat, 100
Crab, 13
  Broad-clawed Porcelain, **88**
  Edible, **88**
  Hermit, **84**
  Shore, **88**
Cranesbill, Bloody, 28, 102, 111
Creeping Jenny, **58**
Crocus, Autumn, 118
Crossbill, 20, 25, 109
Crow, Carrion, **53**, 100
  Crowfoot, 101
  Water, 26, **27**, **74**
crustaceans, **87–88**, *see also* under individual species
Cuckoo, 31, **43**, 100
Cudweed, Marsh, 101
  Small, 103
Curlew, 17, 32, **39**, 106, 109, 111, 119, 120, 121
Cuttlefish, Common, **88**

Dab, 109
Daffodil, Wild, 100, 108
Daisy, **74**
  Ox-eye, 28, **77**
Dandelion, **61**
Dartmoor National Park, 3, 4, 5, 18–20, **18**, 25
Dawlish Warren, 15, 108
Deer, 25
  antler marks of, **25**
  Fallow, 20, 25, 106, 109, 110, 115
  Red, 3, 20, **20**, 25, 105, 120
  Roe, 20, 25, **54**, 106, 110, 115
  Sika, 115, 116
Deer Grass, 18
Dipper, 20, **20**, 110, 119, 120
Diver, Black-throated, 101
  Great Northern, 101
Dock, Shore, 101
Dogwood, 106
Dolphin, **12**, 103
Dormouse, Common, 100
Dove, Collared, **42**
  Rock, **42**, 112
  Stock, **42**
downland, 28, 29
  chalk, 28
  flora of, 29
Dropwort, 28
Duck, Eider, 108
  Long-tailed, 111, 113
  Tufted, **35**, 103
ducks, **35–36**; *see also* under individual species
Dunlin, **16**, 17, 18, **40**, 106, 108, 111
Dunnock, **45**
Durdle Door, **6**

Elm, English, **94**, 96
Eel, 26
estuaries, 5, 10, 16–17
  Avon, 106
  Axe, 16, 110
  Camel, 99
  Char, 16
  Erme, 108
  Exe, 5, 17, 108
  Fal, 5, 17, 100
  Hayle, 101
  Helford, 101
  Kingsbridge, **16**, 109
  Otter, 16, 110
  Parrett, 17
  Poole Harbour, 17, 115
  Tamar, 5, 16, 17, 111
  Taw, Torridge, 17, 111
Eyebright, 98
Exeter, 4
Exmoor National Park, 4, 5, 19, **20**, 25, **25**, 112, 119–120

farming, changes in patterns of, 22
farmland, **8–9**, 22–23
fen, 32

Fern, Adder's Tongue, 99
Brittle Bladder, 118
Royal, **32**, 98, 101, 116
Tunbridge Filmy, 103;
see also Polypody
Fieldfare, **23**, **48**
Fig, Hottentot, **11**
Fir, Douglas, **90**, **96**
European Silver, **90**, **96**
Firecrest, 102
Flag, Yellow, 26, **27**, 101
Flax, Purging, 29, 109
Fleabane, Blue, 104
Flounder, **17**
Flycatcher, 112, 114
Pied, 20, 24, **47**, 102, 108, 118, 119
Spotted, **47**, 107
Forget-me-Not, Common, **62**
forests
Ashclyst Forest, 106
Burrator Forest, 107
Deerpark Forest, 100
Great Haldon (Exeter Forest), 109
Halvana Plantation, 101
Plym Forest, 110
Wareham Forest, 116; *see also* woodland, woods
fossils, 28, 115, 116
mammal, 28; *see also* Ammonite
Fox, 20, 25, 100, 103, 107
Red, **54**
Foxglove, **22**, **68**
Fulmar, 10, **12**, **42**, 101, 104, 106, 109, 114, 115
fungi, 102

Gadwall, 103, 119
Gale, Sweet, 121
Gannet, 106, 111, 114
gardens
Athelhampton Gardens, 114
Clapton Court, 118
Cotehele, 99
Dartington Hall Gardens and Estate, 107
Dunster Castle, 119
Fox Rosehill Gardens, 101
Glendurgan Gardens, 101
Gyllyndgdune Gardens, 101
Kimberley Park Gardens, 101
Lanhydrock, 102
Paignton Zoological and Botanical Gardens, 110
Sub-tropical Gardens, 116
Trelissick, 104
Trengwainton Garden, 103
Garlic, Crow, 106
Wood (also called Ramsons), **72**, 100
geology, 4–6
map, **4**
Gentian, Autumn, 118
Germander, Water, 107
Gipsywort, 101
Glasswort, 17, **17**
Goat, Wild, 112
Goldcrest, 25, **52**
Goldeneye, 34, 101, 108
Golden Rod, **60**
Goldfinch, **51**, 107
Godwit, Bar-tailed, 17, **39**, 108, 111
Black-tailed, **16**, **39**, 100
Goose, Brent, **16**, 108
Canada, **34**
White-fronted, **32**, 99, 121
Gorse, 18, **61**
Dwarf, **31**
European, 30
Western, 18, 30, **30**, 102
granite, 4, **4**, 5
Grass, Bent, 18
Eel, **16**, 108
Marram, **15**
Purple Moor, 18, **20**, 102, 121
Sea Couch, 15
Sea Meadow, 99
Sheep's Fescue, 18
Grasshopper, 30
gravel, 5
Great Haldon, 5, 109
Grebe, Black-necked, 108
Great Crested, **36**, 101, 111, 119
Little, **36**
Red-necked, 101
Slavonian, 101, 108
Greenshank, 17, **40**, 100, 106, 108, 109, 111
Greenweed, Dyer's, 99
Gromwell, Common, 99
Purple, 28
Groundsel, **59**
Grouse, Red, 18, **19**, 119
Guillemot, 10, **12**, **42**, 101, 103, 104, 106, 115
Gulf Stream, 7
Gull, Black-headed, **41**, 104
Common, **41**
Greater Black-backed, 104
Herring, **41**
Lesser Black-backed, **41**
Little, 119
Sabine's, 104

Haldon Hills, 25
Haliclona oculata, **83**
Hare, Brown, **55**, 102
Harebell, 28, **63**, 106
Harrier, 107
Hen, 18
Montagu's, 31, **31**
Hawfinch, **50**
Hawkbit, Lesser, 107
Hawthorn, Common, **95–6**
heath, 18, 30; *see also* heathland
Heath, Cornish, 102
Cross-leaved, 30, 102, 112
Dorset, 30, 31
Heather, **66**
Bell, 18, 30, **30**, **66**, 102, 112
heathland, **8–9**, 30–31, **30**
Hedgehog, **54**
hedges, 22
hedgerows, 22, **33**; flowers of, **22**
Hellebore, 25
Stinking, 106
Helleborine, Marsh, **15**, 107
Herb Bennet, **59**
Herb Paris, 118
Herb Robert, **22**, **66**
Heron, Grey, 17, 20, **36**, 100, 111, 118
heronry, 105, 106, 114
Hobby, 21, 31, 119
Hod Hill, 3, 29, 115
Hogweed, **22**, 24, **74**
Holly, **95–6**
Sea, **11**, 15, 110, 114
Honeysuckle, **22**, **64**
Hoopoe, 102
Hounds-tongue, 101
Hurlstone Point, **13**

Ice Age, 5, 32
Iris, Stinking, 106

Jackdaw, 10, **53**, 106, 112
Jay, **53**
Jellyfish, Moon, **87**
Juniper, **91**, **96**, 102

Kestrel, 10, 18, 20, **37**, 106
Kimmeridge, 5
Kingfisher, **27**, **43**, 107, 108, 109, 110, 120
Kittiwake, 10, 101, 104, 106, 109, 115
Knapweed, Lesser, **67**
Knot, 17, **40**, 108, 111
Knotgrass, **65**

Lady's Mantle, 28
Lady's Smock, **67**
lakes, 26
Beesands, 26
at Cricket St Thomas, 26
Dozmary Pool, 26, 100
Loe Pool and Bar, 26, 102
Radipole Lake, 116
at Sherborne, 26
Siblyback, 27
Slapton Ley, 26, 110
Stithians, 27
Tamar, 27, 111; *see also* reservoirs
Land's End, 3, 4, **5**, 102
landslip, 4, 5
Axmouth-Lyme Regis, 4
Lapwing, 18, 32, **38**, 120, 121
Larch, European, **90**, **96**
Laver, Gut, **83**
leats, 27
Leek, Three-cornered, 10
Lily of the Valley, 25
Lime, Common, **94**, **96**
Small-leaved, 117
limestone, 4, **4**, 5, **6**, 28–29
Carboniferous, 28
fauna of, 29
flora of, 28, 29
Limpet, Blue-rayed, 13
Common, **85**
Slipper, **85**
Ling, 18, 30, **31**, **66**, 102
Linnet, 31, **51**, 106, 107, 108, 110
Little Robin, 99
Lizard, Common, **21**, 102, 104
Sand, **31**, 116
Lizard, the, 4, 10, 102
Lizard Point, 102
Lobster, Common, **88**
Montagu's Plated, **88**
Logan Rock Beach, **14**
Loosestrife, Purple, 26, **27**, 32
Lords and Ladies, 100
Lousewort, 30
lowland, 4–5
Lugworm, 17
Lundy Island, 10
Lupin, Tree, 108
Lyme Regis, 5

Madder, Wild, 25, 99
Mallow, Tree, **11**
Magpie, **53**
Maiden Castle, 3, **28**, 29, 115
Mallard, **35**
Marigold, Marsh, 103
marl, 4, **4**, 5, **5**
Martin, House, **44**
Sand, **44**, 111
Mayweed, Sea, 15
Meadow-rue, Lesser, 118
Meadowsweet, **22**, 32, **74**, 120
Medick, Toothed, 103
Melilot, Common, 103
Golden, 103
Mendips, 4, 22, 25, 28, 121
Mercury, Dog's, 24, **72**
Merganser, Red-breasted, **36**, 101, 108
Merlin, **19**, 107
Milkwort, Common, 18, 30, **62**
Sea, **65**
Mink, 27, **27**
Minehead, 4
mining, 4, **7**
molluscs, **85–86**
Mole, **54**
Moneywort, Cornish, 103
moor, 4, **7**, 18
moorland, **8–9**, 18–21, 30
Moss, Sphagnum, 18, 32, 121
Moth
Burnet, 103, 107
Cinnabar, 107
Drinker, 103
Emperor, **21**, 30, 103
Fox, 30
Oak Eggar, 103
Six-spot Burnet, **11**
Mouse, Wood, **55**
mudflats, **8–9**, 17
Mullein, 106
Mullet, Grey, 109
museums
Brixham Museum, 106
Buckfastleigh Caves, 107
Bude Historical and Folk Exhibition, 99
Budleigh Salterton Museum, 107
Camborne School of Mines, 99
Cheddar Caves Museum and Exhibition, 118
Dairyland and Country Life Museum, 100
Dorset County Museum, 115
Exeter Royal Albert Memorial Museum and Art Gallery, 109
Frome and East Mendip Museum, 120

Geevor Tin Mining Museum, 101
Geological Museum, 103
Ilfracombe Museum, 109
Isles of Scilly Museum, 102
Marine Biological Association, 109
Morwellham Open Air Museum, 109
Penlee House Museum, 103
Philpot Museum, 115
Red House Museum and Art Gallery, 116
St Ives Museum, 104
Somerset County Museum, 121
Teignmouth Museum, 111
Tiverton Museum, 112
Torquay Natural History Society, 112
Truro County Museum, 104
Wells Museum, 121
Mussel, 13
Common, **85**
Horse, **86**
Mustard, Garlic, **72**
Myrtle, Bog, 30

National Parks, *see* Exmoor, Dartmoor
National Nature Reserves
Axmouth-Lyme Regis Landslip, 106
Braunton Burrows, 106
Bridgwater Bay, 117
Ebbor Gorge, 119
The Lizard, 102
Studland Heath, 116
Yarner Wood, 108
nature reserves
Arlington Court, 105
Arne Heath, 113
Aylesbeare and Harpford Commons, 106
Berry Head Country Park, 106
Black Rock Reserve, 118
Black Venn, 114
Brownsea Island, 114
Buckfastleigh Caves, 107
Chardown, Stonebarrow and the Undercliffs, 114
Coombe Valley, 99
Dawlish Warren, 108
Dunsford Nature Reserve, 107
Fontmell Downs, 115
Hangingcliff Woods, 111
Hemyock, Ashculm Turbary, 109
Hurscombe Reserve, 119
Lundy Island, 109
Pendarves Wood, 103
Purbeck Marine Wildlife Reserve, 115
Radipole Lake, 116
Saltern Cove, 112
Sidmouth Cliffs, 110
The Spittles, 116
Tiverton Canal, 106
Velvet Bottom, 118
Ventongimps Moor, 104
Welcombe Mouth, 112
Whitenothe Cliff, 116
Woody Bay, 112; *see also* National Nature Reserves
nature trails
Aisholt Ring Walk, 121
Ammderdown Nature Trail, 117
Black Rock Nature Trail, 118
Castle Neroche Nature Trail, 118
Cloutsham Nature Trail, 118
Hurscombe Nature Trail, 119
Long Wood Nature Trail, 118
Quantock Forest Walk, 121
Necklace Shell, **86**
Nettle, **75**
White Dead, **75**
Nightjar, 31, **31**, 106, 109, 113, 119
Nightshade, Black, **78**
Enchanter's, 20, 24
Woody, **70**
Nuthatch, 20, **50**, 106, 107, 108, 110, 118

Oak, coppiced, 24
English, **91**, **96**
Sessile, **92**, **96**
Oakwood, 24, 30
Oarweed, 13
Old Man's Beard, 28, **60**
Orchid, Bee, 29, **29**
Butterfly, 29
Early Marsh, 101
Early Purple, **69**, 104, 109
Early Spider, 29
Frog, 29
Fuschia, 102
Heath Spotted, 30
Lesser Butterfly, 102
Man, 29
Pyramidal, 29, 101
Southern Marsh, **32**
Spotted, 29
orchids, 29, 106, 109, 115
Oriole, Golden, 102
Otter, 27, **27**, **56**
Ouzel, Ring, **19**, 112, 119, 120
Owl, Barn, **23**, **43**
Little, 32, **43**
Long-eared, **43**
Short-eared, 18, 32, **43**, 107, 113
Tawny, **43**, 106
Oyster, Common, **85**
Saddle, **85**
Oystercatcher, 15, 17, **38**, 103, 106, 108, 109, 111, 117, 120

Pansy, Seaside, 107
Wild, **61**
Parsley, Cow, **73**
Knotted Bur, 102, 104
Upright Hedge, **73**
Partridge, **37**
Pea, Sea, 110, 114
Pearlwort, Heath, 98
Sea, 101, 107
peat, 18, 32
moors, Somerset, 121
Pellitory-of-the-wall, **77**
Pennywort, Marsh, 101
Wall, **23**, 28
Perch, 26
Peregrine, 3, **11**, 106, 109, 112, 120
Periwinkle, Common (mollusc), **85**
Flat, **86**
Periwinkle (flower), 13
Lesser, **63**
Petrel, Leach's, 104
Storm, 101, 104
Pheasant, **37**
Pike, 26
Pillwort, 102
Pimpernel, Bog, 101
Scarlet, **71**
Yellow, **59**
Pine, Chile, **91**, **96**
Corsican, **90**, **96**
Maritime, **89**, **96**
Scots, **89**, **96**
Pink, Cheddar, 28, 118
Sea, 102
Pintail, **35**, 99, 111, 116
Pipit, Meadow, 18, **31**, **45**, 119
Rock, 103
Tree, **45**, 106, 118
Plaintain, Buckshorn, 101, 102
Greater, **78**
Hoary, 28
Lesser Water, 101, 104
Ribwort, **78**
Sea, 102
Plover, Golden, 3, 18, **19**, 101
Grey, 99, 101, 108
Ringed, 17, **38**, 108, 113, 117, 120
Plymouth, 4, 28
Pochard, **36**, 116
Policeman's Helmet (also called Himalayan Balsam), **68**
Polypody, Common, **23**
Limestone, 118
Poole Harbour, 3, 17, 115
Ponies, **18**
Shetland, 105
Poppy, Common, 104
Field, **71**
Long-headed, **71**
Yellow Horned, 15, **15**, 101, 110
porpoise, 102
Portland, 10, 22, 29
Bill of, 114
Prawle Point, 5, **5**
Prawn, Common, **88**
Primrose, **23**, **59**
Puffin, 10, **12**, 25, 26, **42**, 48, 101, 109
puffinry, 103
Purbeck, 22, 29, 30
Isle of, 115
Purslane, Water, 101

Quantocks, 25, 30, 121
Quantoxhead, East, 5, 119
Quillwort, Sand, 102

Rabbit, **55**, 107
Radish, Sea, 110
Ragged Robin, **67**
Ragworm, 17
Ragwort, **61**
Rail, Water, 27
rainfall, 7
Ramsons (also called Wood Garlic), **72**, 100
Rape, **61**
Rattle, Yellow, **58**
Raven, 10, **19**, 20, 101, 104, 107, 108, 111
Razorbill, 10, **12**, 101, 103, 104, 115
Razorshell, 15, **15**, 86
Redpoll, 20, 25, **25**, 109, 119
Lesser, **51**
Redshank, **16**, 17, 32, **38**, 106, 108, 109, 119, 121
Spotted, 17, 108, 111, 119
Redstart, 20, 24, 32, **48**, 100, 102, 106, 119
Black, 115
Redwing, **48**
Reed, 26
Reed-mace, 26
Great, 101
reservoirs, 26
Burrator, 107
Clatworthy, 118
Durleigh, 119
Wimbleball Lake, 119
Rest-harrow, 15, 104, 110
rhine, 32, **32**
rivers, 26–27
Robin, **48**
Rocket, Sea, 106, 114, 115
Rockrose Common, **58**, 106, 118
White, 28, **29**, 106, 117
Rook, **53**
Rose, Dog, **22**, **64**
Downy, 103
Rowan, 20, **92**, **96**
Rudd, 26
Ruff, **40**, 108, 119
Rupturewort, Ciliate, 102
Rush, Sea, 107
Sea Club, 99

St Austel, 4
St John's Wort, Common, **57**
St Michael's Mount, **3**, 103
Sallow, 30
Salmon, 26, 107
saltmarsh, **8–9**, 16, 17
Saltwort, 104
Prickly, 101
Samphire, Common, 99
Golden, **11**, 99
Rock, 10, **11**, 102, 111, 118
sand dunes, **8–9**, 15
Sanderling, **40**, 106, 108
Sand Gaper, 17
Common, **86**
Sandpiper, Common, 20, **38**, 99, 101
Curlew, 99, 100, 108
Green, 119
Wood, 119
sandstone, 4, **4**, 5, **5**, **6**
Old Red, 121
Sandwort, Sea, **77**, 116
Sanicle, 100
Scabious, Devil's Bit, **69**
Field, **69**

Scaup 111
schist 4 **4** 5 **6**
Scoter 114
Seablite 17 114
Sea Hare **14**
Sea Kale 110 114
Seal Common **56**
Grey **12** **56** 99 101 103
Sanctuary Cornish 101
Sea Lavender **11** 17 **70** 111 114
Rock 102
Sea Lettuce **83**
sea level changes in 5 16
Sea Oak **83**
Sea Potato **87**
Sea Slug 13 **14**
Sea Squirt 13
Sea Urchin 15
Edible **87**
seaweeds **83**
brown 13; *see also* under individual species
Sedge Sand 107 108
serpentine 4
Service Wild 109 117
Shag 10 **34** 101 104 106
shale 4 **4** **6**
Shark Basking 99
Common Blue 102
Mako 102
Porbeagle 102
Shearwater Balearic 114
Manx 109 114
Sooty 104
Sheep Jacob 105
Shelduck **36** 100 106 107 108 109 118 119
shells **85–86**; *see also* under individual species
Shepherd's Purse **75**
shingle 5
shore exposed 13
rocky 4 **8–9** 10 13 **13**
sandy **8–9** 10 15
sheltered 13
Shoreweed 107
Shoveler **35** 103 116
Shrew Common **55**
Shrimp Sand **88**
White **88**
Silverweed **60**
Siskin **50** 109
Skua Arctic 104
Skylark 18 29 **45** 114 119
Slapton Sands 5 15 110
slate 4 **4** 5
Smew 113
Snake Grass 31
Smooth 116
Snipe 18 **20** 31 **40** 121
Somerset Levels **9** 32 **32** 121
Sorrel Wood 20 **77**
Sparrow House **52**
Tree **52**
Sparrowhawk 103 106 118
Spearwort Lesser 101
Speedwell Common **62**
Spikenard Ploughman's 104
Spindle 100
Sponge 13
Bread-crumb **83**
Spruce Norway **89** **96**
Sitka **89** **96**
Spurge Portland 101 107
Spurrey Corn **76**
Rock 99
Rock Sea 102
Sand **65** 104
Sea 101
Squill Autumn 111
Spring **11** 99 111
Squinancywort 29
Squirrel feeding place of **25**
Grey **55**
Red **55** 114
Starfish **14** 15
Common **87**
Starling **48** 111
Start Point 4 5 10
Starwort Water 100
Stint Little 99 101 108
Stitchwort Greater **72**
Stoat 20 **56** 100 103
Stonechat 18 **19** 31 106 107 108 111 113 120
Stonecrop Biting **23** 28
Storksbill Sea 107 108
Strawberry Wild **73** 100
Studland 15
Sucker Fish Cornish 103
Sundew Common 32 98 121
Round-leaved **21**
Sunstar **87**
Swallow **44** 111
Swan Bewick's 32 121
Mute **34** 113
Swannery Abbotsbury 113
Swift **44**
Sycamore 20 24 **94** **96**

Taunton 4
Teal **35** 101 103 111 120
Teasel Wild 10 **69**
Teignmouth 4
Tellin 17
Baltic **86**
Tern Common **41** 113 114
Little **41** 113 114
ternery 114
terns 108
Thistle Carline 106 111
Musk 29
Thrift 10 **10** **65**
Thrush Mistle **49**
Song **49**
Thyme 10 106
tides 17
Tit 20
Bearded 116
Blue **49**
Coal **49**
Great **49**
Long-tailed **49**
Marsh **49** 120
Toadflax Ivy-leaved **23** **70**
Prostrate 103
Topshell Painted **85** 102
tor 5 18 20
Torbay 4 28 112
Tormentil 18 21 30
Torquay 4
Treecreeper 20 **50** 106 107 110 118
Trefoil Bird's Foot 10 **60** 103 106 110
Trough Shell Rayed **86**
Trout Brown 26
Sea 26 107
turf cliff-top **10**
Turnstone **38**
Twayblade Common 100

upland 4

Valerian **68**
Red **23** 114
Vetch Horseshoe 28 29
Kidney 10 106
Tufted **22** **70**
Wood 98
Violet Common Dog **69**
Hairy 102 107
Vole Short-tailed **55**
Water **56**
waders 17 **38–40**; *see also* under individual species
Wagtail Grey 20 **20** **45** 120
Pied **45**
Yellow 32 **45** 121
walls stone 22 **23**
Warbler 106
Garden **46**
Cetti's 26 110
Dartford 31 **31** 110 113
Grasshopper 113 118
Reed 26 **46** 110 116 119
Sedge 26 32 **46** 110 116
Willow **46**
Wood 20 **47** 108 112 119
Water-lily 26
White 103
Yellow 103
Water Dropwort Hemlock 120
Watermint **69**
Waterthrush Northern 102
Weasel 20 **56** 104
Weever Fish Lesser 99
Westward Ho! 5
Whale 103
Wheatear **19** 20 **47** 99 100 107 108 112 120
Whelk Common **85**
Dog 13 **13** **85**
Netted Dog **85**
Whimbrel **39** 106 111
Whinchat 18 32 **47** 120
Whitethroat **46** 108 110 120
Wigeon **16** 17 **35** 103 108 119
wildfowl refuge
Arlington Court 105
Radipole Lake 116
Tamar Lakes 111
wildlife parks; *see* zoos
Willow Creeping 107
Dwarf 30
Goat **93** **96**
pollarded 32
White **93** **96**
Willowherb Great **65**
Rosebay **66**
Wintergreen Round-leaved **15**
Woodcock **39**
woodland **8–9** 20 24–25 **24** **25**
broadleaved 20
coniferous 20
on Dartmoor 20
deciduous 24
wet 32; *see also* forests woods
Woodpecker 20 24 106 108 110 111 118
Greater Spotted **44**
Green 29 **44**
Lesser Spotted **44**
Woodpigeon **42**
Woodrush 24
woods
Cardinham Woods 99
Cranborne Chase 115
Dunmere Wood 100
Horner Woods 119
Pendarves Wood 103
Peter's Wood 103
Shaptor Woods 108
Thorncombe Wood 116
Yarner Wood 108
Woody Bay 10
Woolacombe Sands 5
Woundwort Wood **71**
Wrack Bladder 13 **83**
Channelled 13 **83**
Knotted 13
Serrated 13
Spiral 13
Wren **46** 99

Acknowledgements: Photographers and Artists

Photographs and paintings are credited by page, left to right, running down the page.

Cover: Geoffrey Kinns, John Mason, E. O. Fellowes, Charles Woolf, D. Hosking, (painting) Chris Shields/Wilcock Riley, Charles Woolf.
Back Cover: John Sibbick/John Martin Artists.

Page 1: R. Mearns. *Page 3:* A. W. Besley. *Page 4:* (map) Swanston Associates. *Page 5:* Charles Woolf, Exeter Museum. *Page 6:* Tony Thomas, Ian Mercer, Exeter Museum, June Chatfield, Mark Wilson. *Page 7:* R. Jarman, Tony Thomas, Tom Grant. *Pages 8–9:* (map) Swanston Associates. *Page 10:* Charles Woolf. *Page 11:* M. C. F. Proctor, Heather Angel, N. A. Callow/NHPA, Charles Woolf, John Mason, Heather Angel, Exeter Museum, Frank Blackburn. *Page 12:* Robert Smith, J. Tallon/NHPA, R. H. Bridson, J. Good/NHPA, B. S. Turner, Stanley Davies/RSPB, A. Butler/NHPA. *Page 13:* J. H. Crothers, J. H. Crothers. *Page 14:* L. Jackman, J. Goodman/NHPA, Heather Angel, A. W. Besley, Robert Estall. *Page 15:* June Chatfield, Mark Wilson, M. C. F. Proctor, Roger Hosking, John Breeds, Exeter Museum. *Page 16:* Ian Mercer, A. J. Bond/Aquila, Michael W. Richards/RSPB, Eric Soothill/Aquila, Stanley Davies/RSPB, Rod Powley/Aquila. *Page 17:* S. C. Bisserot, J. Goodman/NHPA, John Breeds, Bain/Cambridge/NHPA. *Page 18:* Ian Mercer. *Page 19:* Jim Parkin, B. Hawkes/NHPA, J. F. Young, C. Linford/Aquila, J. F. Young, Frank Blackburn. A. T. Moffett/Aquila, A. T. Moffett/ Aquila. *Page 20:* B. Hawkes/NHPA, S. Kill/Aquila, D. Avon & T. Tilford, J. Good/NHPA, B. S. Turner. *Page 21:* D. A. Smith, John Breeds, John Breeds, A. T. Moffett/ Aquila, P. Sterry, John Mason, Heather Angel, Heather Angel, Mark Wilson, Heather Angel. *Page 22:* (painting) John Sibbick/John Martin Artists. *Page 23:* D. Horne, Roger Hosking, D. N. Dalton/NHPA, F. Blackburn/Aquila, Martin Davies /RSPB Tony Thomas, (painting) John Sibbick/John Martin Artists. *Page 24:* Ian Mercer. *Page 25:* R. Mearns, John Breeds, D. Avon & T. Tilford, Rosamund Kidman Cox (bottom three photographs). *Page 26:* Ian Mercer. *Page 27:* Margaret Wood, John Birks, E. O. Fellowes, Ian Mercer, John Breeds, Ian Mercer. *Page 28:* M. C. F. Proctor. *Page 29:* S. C. Bisserot, Geoffrey Kinns, John Mason, Ros Evans, Mark Wilson, Heather Angel, Mark Wilson. *Page 30:* Charles Woolf. *Page 31:* A. Cundall/Aquila, J. F. Young, Stanley Davies/RSPB, Heather Angel, John Breeds, Stanley Davies/RSPB, John Breeds. *Page 32:* R. Jarman, R. Jarman, Mark Wilson, Mark Wilson, Exeter Museum. *Page 33:* John Sibbick/John Martin Artists. *Pages 34–53:* Trevor Boyer. *Page 54:* Chris Shields/ Wilcock Riley. *Page 55:* David Wright/Tudor Art, Chris Shields/Wilcock Riley. *Page 56:* Chris Shields/Wilcock Riley. *Pages 57–70:* Hilary Burn. *Page 71:* Hilary Burn, Michelle Emblem/Middletons, Hilary Burn. *Pages 72–8* Hilary Burn. *Pages 79–80:* Joyce Bee. *Page 81:* Joyce Bee, Chris Shields/Wilcock Riley. *Page 82:* Joyce Bee. *Pages 83–5:* John Barber, Michelle Emblem/Middletons. *Pages 87–8:* John Barber. *Pages 89–95:* Annabel Milne & Peter Stebbing. *Page 96:* Annabel Milne & Peter Stebbing, Bob Bampton/Garden Studio (Hawthorn). *Page 97:* A. F. Kersting. Maps on pages 98, 105, 113, 117: Swanston Associates *Page 122:* (drawing) Andy Martin.